IS IOWA HAUNTED?

Would you dare to sit in the haunted Devil's Chair or to shake hands with the Black Angel? *Even if it meant your imminent death?*

Here's the definitive guide for finding . . .

- The ghosts of Buddy Holly, Richie Valens, and the Big Bopper

- Ghosts who push your car

- Phantom hitchhikers

- Specters who grant wishes

- Banshees

- The Grim Reaper

- Statues that come to life

- Headless ghosts

- Phantom trains

- Haunted trees

- Disappearing houses

- Ghost children

- The haunted 13 steps

- A portal to Heaven

Visit haunted airports, bridges, cemeteries, historic homes, libraries, lover's leaps, museums, parks, police stations, restaurants, roads, and theatres.

Encounter the ghosts of football players, generals, Gypsies, hillbillies, Indians, outlaws, pirates, prisoners, slaves, soldiers, thieves, and wrestlers.

WHAT PEOPLE ARE SAYING ABOUT THIS BOOK

"In the aboriginal tongue, 'I-o-way' means, 'This is the place.' One may readily ask, 'The place for what?' and suggest, 'For cows, pigs, lots of corn fields, prairie grass, and gently rolling hills.' But now in this remarkable road guide, Terry Fisk and Chad Lewis declare that Iowa is the place to find ghosts— and lots of them, from one corner of the state to the other. As someone who has trekked the state for well over 50 years in search of real ghosts, restless spirits, and haunted places, I can attest to Fisk and Lewis having guided the spook seeker to every notable eerie site in the Hawkeye state. In addition, our trusty guides have discovered some shadowy corners that I hadn't previously explored and that I will be certain to add to the itinerary of my next psychic safari."

Brad Steiger - Author/co-author of 164 books on the paranormal and things that go bump in the night; resident of Forest City, IA.

****

"Before you stop at that B&B tonight, better check whether a ghost will be staying in an adjoining room. Likewise, wading in that woodland stream or wandering though that overgrown graveyard could be dangerous. Is there a restless soul loose on the premises? The newest guidebook from the Unexplained team—this time for your back road wanderings through Iowa— is not only the indispensable Baedeker for those who search out the supernatural in old hotels, filling stations, theaters, bridges, bogs and marshes, but it is also the caveat of caution for those who would rather not meet up with someone's murdered girlfriend. Tantalizing ghostly secrets are here in this book, which provides the locations and the directions to finding Iowa's mysterious locales. Fun and readable as only a good guide book can be, The Iowa Road Guide to Haunted Locations *presents all the intriguing folklore and folktales but—for the skeptical among you—provides sterner research debunking all the old superstitions while leaving The Unexplained for the traveler still to discover."*

Lara Parker - Author of the *Dark Shadows* novels: *Angelique's Descent* and *The Salem Branch;* studied drama at the University of Iowa; played Angelique on ABC TV's *Dark Shadows.*

THE
IOWA
ROAD GUIDE
TO
HAUNTED
LOCATIONS

To
Stacy –
Sleep with the
lights on!

[signature]

THE
IOWA
ROAD GUIDE
TO
HAUNTED
LOCATIONS

By Chad Lewis & Terry Fisk

UNEXPLAINED

Research Publishing Company

A Division of Unexplained Research, LLC

Library of Congress Control Number: 2006903789
ISBN-13: 978-0-9762099-4-2
ISBN-10: 0-9762099-4-2

Printed in the United States by McNaughton & Gunn, Inc.

Unexplained Research Publishing Company
A Division of Unexplained Research LLC
P.O. Box 2173, Eau Claire, WI 54702-2173
Email: info@unexplainedresearch.com
www.unexplainedresearch.com

Cover Design: Terry Fisk
Back Cover Photo: Rob Mattison

DEDICATION

I dedicate this book to my father, Bill Lewis, who wisely appreciates the beauty of undeveloped land, much like the people of Iowa.

—Chad

I dedicate this book to my Iowa roots: the Fisks, Wiesenders, Hoaglans, and Dennisons.

—Terry

TABLE OF CONTENTS

2 - Northwest Iowa   97

3 - Southeast Iowa   173

4 - Southwest Iowa   211

PREFACE

Corrections. Although we have made every effort to be certain that this road guide is reliable and accurate, things inevitably change and errors are made. We appreciate it if readers contact us so we can revise future editions of the book.

Updates. If you have a paranormal experience at one of these locations, please report it to us. We recommend that you keep a journal, carefully recording dates, times, locations, and what happened.

Additions. Due to lack of space, many locations had to be left out the book. We do intend to publish a second volume. Please write and let us know of any Iowa locations that you feel should have been included in this travel guide.

Warning. Be respectful of both the living and the dead. Several communities have had problems with people who go to these locations only to party and cause mischief. Cemeteries have been desecrated, private property has been vandalized, grounds have been littered, and buildings have been broken into.

If you do decide to check out any of the locations for yourself, please make sure that you have permission if it is private property and obey all applicable laws. Under most ordinances, cemeteries are only open from sunrise to sunset.

We will not be held responsible for any persons who decide to conduct their own investigations or for those who choose to break laws.

Disclaimer. The places listed in the book have neither been proved nor disproved to be haunted. Their inclusion in the book is based on the anecdotal reports we have received from numerous individuals. This book is for reference purposes only.

FOREWORD

I don't know what it is about human nature but apparently a number of us like to be scared now and then. After all, that's why we go to scary movies, watch scary television shows and pick up books like the one you're reading right now, right? You're doing this because there's something about ghosts that intrigues us—are they real or aren't they?

For those of us who haven't seen ghosts, or even if we have (I think I encountered one in the middle of the night years ago, although I saw nothing but certainly experienced something pushing by me in the dark), we're interested in the stories and lore of those who say they have. For some of us, just hearing or reading the stories about ghostly encounters is good enough to set our hair on end and that's what is neat about the books by Chad Lewis and Terry Fisk.

I'm not sure why Chad and Terry began looking into tales of the unexplained but I'm glad they're publishing their results.

Occasionally they state that some tales are just that—tales and nothing more—stories that have been told about certain places and events that just didn't take place as rumored. No one hanged himself here. No one by that name ever lived here. Nothing ever burned to the ground here.

But then they have those tales that are unexplained. Some people they have interviewed report being bumped in the night by something invisible. Others saw apparitions float by. A door that was unlocked a moment ago is now locked. The smell of tobacco is present although no one else is around. The bell in an empty church rings. The lights go out.

Funny thing, often when I read those tales, I'm okay. It's later when I think back upon reading those tales, like when I'm trying to go to sleep, that I feel haunted by them and shiver.

One thing that I like about Chad and Terry's work is that they don't do like so many other ghost book authors do: "Somewhere in the eastern part of the state, near a small winding stream was a mansion built before the turn of the century." I've read passages like that over the years and frankly I tire of them and question if a sighting reported like that ever took place.

Instead, Chad and Terry tell it exactly like it is. They state where the sightings occurred, complete with addresses, phone numbers and directions (plus proper warnings to not trespass and respect private property)—wow, just what people like me would like in case I'm traveling near where sightings have been reported—a chance to see a place where people have encountered something that has no explanation. To me, that lends credibility—and spookiness too—to those sightings that cannot be explained. Who could ask for more?

—Mike Whye
Author of *Great Iowa Weekend Adventures* and *The Great Iowa Touring Book.*

PS. My 15-year-old daughter just told me that her 17-year-old brother said he had just read another *Haunted Locations* book by Chad and Terry and called it "creepy." Now, that's a recommendation!

ACKNOWLEDGMENTS

We would like to thank Nisa Giaquinto, Brad Bryan, Sarah Szymanski, Paul Stucklen, and Jeannine Fisk for assisting us with the research and production of this book.

We also want to thank the many people who provided us with cases, directions, and personal accounts.

INTRODUCTIONS

The universe will reward you for taking risks on its behalf.

—*Shakti Gawain*

The national media like to portray Iowa as a state where the only things to do are watching the corn grow and chasing tornadoes. Even if you enjoy partaking in these activities, Iowa provides many more adventures for those simply looking to seek them out. Besides being the state that holds the American Gothic House, the Field of Dreams movie site, the National Hobo Convention, the childhood home of John Wayne, and the world's largest Cheeto, Iowa is filled with many more sinister places for you to visit. Although the state is relatively small in size, it is packed with so many ghosts that you will not have to venture far to seek out your own paranormal experience.

Most of you have probably seen one of the numerous TV shows about ghosts on the Discovery Channel or The Learning Channel. Although it is fun to hear about hauntings in other places in other states, it is a whole other matter when these places are in your own backyard. This book makes visiting these places easy because we took care of all the hard work. We scoured the records for the real history of places, dug up the ghost lore, recorded eyewitness accounts, conducted our own investigations, captured photos of the sites, and even provided you with directions on how to get there. We have left the big choice up to you as to whether you want to read about the cases from the safety of your own home, or if you would rather visit these places for yourself. But please beware, going to these places is much different from watching them on TV because when you are in a haunted cemetery and you see shadowy figure lurking from gravestone to gravestone you cannot simply change the channel. When you hear the unearthly moan of children eternally trapped at their place of death, the mute button will do you no good.

I am often asked: "What equipment do I need to start my adventure?" To begin your ghost adventure you will need two simple things, a good dose of curiosity and the book you are holding in your hands. You may also want add a camera to your arsenal to capture that floating ball of light or to provide the police who find your frightened-to-death body some clues as to what happened to you. Everything else is just icing on the cake, or more aptly put, dirt on the coffin. Do not let the fact that you haven't spent thousands of dollars on equipment impede you on your adventure. Many of the best investigations were conducted with the simplest of devices. If you find that you need more equipment you can always pick it up as you go.

For me, this book is as much about adventure as it is about ghosts. This is your cure for the "there-is-nothing-to-do" boredom that haunts us all. There is nothing more exciting than grabbing a friend, your new book, and setting out on your very own adventure. This is your chance to get out and explore your state. Trust me, while you are on this adventure you will meet some odd people, see many odd things, find local lore, and discover that Iowa is much more bizarre than you could have ever imagined.

Good luck on your adventure,

Chad Lewis

There are two kinds of adventurers; those who go truly hoping to find adventure and those who go secretly hoping they won't.

—*Rabindranath Tagore*

My roots are in Iowa. In 1869, in an effort to encourage immigration, the state printed a 96-page booklet entitled, *Iowa: The Home of Immigrants.* The booklet was published in English, but there was also a German language version distributed to Germany. This created an influx of immigrants which included my German ancestors in the Wiesender family. Both my paternal and maternal ancestors came from Iowa. On my father's side of the family, the Fisks had settled in western Iowa. On my mother's side, the Wiesenders, Hoaglans, and Dennisons had lived in the counties of Buchanan and Clayton in eastern Iowa. Two or three generations later, my parents met, fell in love, and were married at the Little Brown Church in the Vale in Nashua, Iowa.

Several years ago, I was researching my ancestors George and Eliza Jane Fisk who were from Lawler County, Iowa. While visiting the cemetery where they were buried, I photographed their headstone. Immediately after, I had my brother Rick snap a picture of me standing next to the grave and later was shocked to discover an unexplained anomaly had been captured in the image. To my amazement, swirling orbs of light and a bluish-white vapor appeared to be rising from the grave and enveloping me. At the time the photo was taken, it was a clear, sunny day. There was no mist, smoke, or fog that could account for this oddity. In fact, the first picture of the grave, taken just a moment earlier, was perfectly normal. I had taken hundreds of photos with that camera, and I found it curious that the only time something strange appeared in a photo, it just happened to be in a cemetery and next to a grave.

This was the event that led me to become a paranormal investigator. I had the photo examined by photography and camera experts, but none of them could explain the anomaly. It was examined by the world-famous debunker James Randi, and even he admitted he couldn't explain it. I wondered if it could actually be possible to capture photographic evidence of spirits, and started venturing out into the cemeteries every night, snapping photos, and hoping to record something strange.  Eventually I met paranormal investigator Chad Lewis, and we began traveling to haunted locations throughout the Midwest. Often, while searching for these haunted hotspots, we found the directions we were given were either vague or completely wrong. There were many times when we ended up totally lost and wasted several hours just driving around in circles. One of us flippantly made the comment that it sure would be convenient if we had a road guide to these haunted locations, and it was at that moment that we decided that we should be the ones to write that book. That decision resulted in the book that you now hold in your hands.

Since that day, Chad and I have made several trips across the Midwest in search of "the unexplained," and Iowa is definitely one of our favorite states. Undeniably, it is a paranormal hotspot with an overabundance of weird things—which is what we thrive on! For over a hundred years people have been reporting strange phenomena in the Hawkeye State.

As far back as the 1880s, a farm family living near Oskaloosa, Iowa saw a UFO that was "lit up like a birthday cake." It flew over their farmhouse and appeared to land behind a nearby hill. The family was terrified and slept in their cellar that night. The next day they mustered all their courage and proceed out to investigate the landing site. Beyond the hill they found a large circular impression in the grass field. There were also some scattered scorch marks. Many of the neighbors had also witnessed the mysterious flying object and were able to corroborate the story. This is the earliest known report of a crop circle in the United States.

In 1893, residents of Scranton, Iowa encountered a 40-foot sea serpent that crawled out of the Coon River west of town. It is said that during its "reign of terror" the creature devoured hogs, calves, and colts.

In 1897, it was reported that a UFO made a stopover landing outside of Waterloo to make repairs.

In 1948, one of the rare cases of spontaneous human combustion (SHC) was reported in Sioux City, Iowa. During the night, Paul Weekley woke up with an itchy leg that suddenly burst into flames. He extinguished the flames and fell asleep on his couch but was awaken again when he felt his leg on fire a second time.

In 1966, Ronald E. Johnson, a farmer living in Yorktown, Iowa, contacted authorities to report a cigar-shaped object, approximately 60 feet in length, had landed in his field. A series of circular impressions were later found at the landing site.

In 1979, a series of Bigfoot sightings in Dallas County had the Iowa authorities combing the woods in search of the 7-foot-tall creature.

Throughout the 1970s, there were several mysterious cattle mutilations on farms across the state. People attributed them to either satanic cults or extraterrestrials. In 2003, Des Moines police investigated another case; this time of a mutilated horse.

Even the Little Brown Church in the Vale, where my parents were married, has a bizarre history. In the 1800s, a young music teacher named William Pitts was traveling from Wisconsin to Iowa to visit his future wife. During a stopover in Nashua, he noticed a vacant lot surrounded by trees and imagined this would be a beautiful location for a church. After returning home, he was inspired to a song, "Church in the Wildwood," with lyrics that described a "little brown church in the vale." The song ended up stashed away in a drawer and forgotten. Many years later, Pitts was again traveling through the Nashua area and was astounded to see a little brown church had been built on that very spot. The parishioners could only afford the least expensive paint, which happened to be brown.

Chad and I have had many adventures in Iowa. Some were strange; others were humorous. During one excursion, we were driving down a rural back road during a torrential rainstorm. Although Chad swears he was driving the speed limit, it seemed like we were going 90 mph. The road had been a long, flat, straight line for several miles, and, because of the limited visibility, Chad failed to see that the road ended abruptly ahead at a T intersection. He hit the brakes, the car went into a skid, we barely missed hitting a sign (actually, it ripped off his side mirror), and the car became airborne.

My memory is a little fuzzy at this point. I don't recall if we yelled, "yeee-haw" like the Dukes of Hazzard or if we just screamed like little girls. Regardless, the car went flying, cleared the ditch, and cut a path about 100 feet long into a field of six-foot-tall corn. When the car finally came to a stop, it was stuck in the mud and buried under a canopy of sheared-off cornstalks. Somehow we managed to push the car out of the cornfield, but both of us ended up caked in mud. The car was covered with corn, but still drivable, so we drove to a nearby town to get washed up. I assure you the convenience store there wasn't too thrilled when we walked in and sullied their establishment. In the restroom, we cleaned ourselves up as best we could, but in the process we left behind a filthy mess. To exit the store we had to slink past an angry clerk who was heavily cursing under his breath while mopping up our footprints. As we hightailed it out of there, we saw something that made us stop dead in our tracks and burst into side-splitting laughter. A flock of crows had gathered on top of our car, and they were eating the corn.

So, hit the road. Have fun, but at the same time be respectful of both the living and the dead. Most importantly, drive carefully and don't take any shortcuts through the Iowa cornfields.

With Metta,

Terry Fisk

IN MEMORIAM

JORDI
The brave little Jardine's Parrot who went to Iowa in search of Phantom Pirates

NORTHEAST IOWA

Holy Cross Cemetery

Location: Anamosa, Jones County, Iowa

Directions: Take Main Street West as it turns into Iowa Street. Turn right on Sage Street and the cemetery will be straight ahead.

Ghost Lore

Cemeteries certainly do not need any assistance in gaining a reputation for being a hotbed for ghosts. Most cemeteries are thought to be haunted by someone buried inside. Now imagine a cemetery that contains an ominous tree that is said to have been used for many hangings and you have a great story for a graveyard haunting. This is actually the background story for the Holy Cross Cemetery.

- An unknown shadow figure lurks in the cemetery.

- An eerie Grim Reaper roams the cemetery searching for souls to harvest.

History

1842 – According to *The History of Jones County,* the town of Anamosa was named after a female Native American visitor.

1893 – A plat book shows the cemetery did operate during this time.

1993 – The recording of Holy Cross Cemetery headstones took place.

Investigation

There are several graves from the 1800s located in the cemetery.

We spoke with a woman who had heard that if you go out to the cemetery at night you will see unexplained burn marks on the tree. The phantom burns are said to be from hangings that took place at the tree years ago. We were unable to find any evidence to support or deny that hangings once took place at the old tree in the cemetery.

A woman told us that her boyfriend was interested in the story of a Reaper in Holy Cross Cemetery so he worked up the courage to visit the cemetery one evening. Not expecting anything to happen, the young man was about to exit the cemetery when he noticed a figure that looked exactly like a Reaper. However, the puzzled young man did not stay around long enough to investigate.

Visitors to the cemetery are often surprised when they see small balls of light, or orbs, floating through the cemetery.

Towards the end of the road that runs through the cemetery sits a large lone tree overlooking the turnaround. Local lore tells of this creepy tree being the site of several tragic hangings that took place in years past. Evidence of these deaths is said to be forever engraved in the still visible rope burns decorating the tree. We were unable to determine the validity of any hangings at the tree.

Rope burns are not the only odd things people see at the tree as a strange unknown shadowy figure has also been spotted lurking about.

Cedar Rapids Public Library

Location: Cedar Rapids, Linn County, Iowa
Address: 500 First Street Southeast, Cedar Rapids, IA
52401-2002
Phone: (319) 398-5123
Office Fax: (319) 398-0476
Reference Fax: (319) 398-0408
Website: www.crlibrary.org

Ghost Lore

The library is a popular place for the community to hold meetings, check out books, rent videos, hear speakers, and even conduct paranormal research. With so many things to do at the library it comes as no surprise that some people do not want to leave. The Cedar Rapids Public Library has a library regular who refuses to leave. What's worse, this unwanted guest is dead.

- The ghost of a library patron continues to visit the library.

- Library items often fly off the shelf for no apparent reason.

History

1890 – The start of the movement to get a public library in Cedar Rapids began.

1896 – The residents of Cedar Rapids voted for a library in town.

1984 – The old library closed.

1985 – The new library opened in its current location.

Investigation

The book *Ghosts of Linn County* reports that Helen Stein was an elderly lady who visited the library on a regular basis. The woman came to the library to read the daily newspaper and talked with the

library staff. One morning Helen came into the library wearing a much nicer dress than the staff was accustomed to seeing her in. The librarian also noticed that she was without her unusual stiff walk. Later that day a man informed the library staff of the sad death of Helen. Immediately the librarians refused to believe him, telling him that they had just seen her at the library and could even describe her dress. The librarians were baffled when they found out that Helen did die in a fire and she was buried in the same dress they saw her wear into the library many hours after her death.

We spoke with a librarian who informed us that this event took place many years ago and that she had not had a paranormal experience.

One librarian did report that several staff members have had odd things happen to them including hearing strange noises and having items misplaced. Some of the staff attributed these events to non-paranormal causes.

Tillie of Oak Hill Cemetery

Location: Cedar Rapids, Linn County, Iowa
Address: 1705 Mount Vernon Road Southeast,
Cedar Rapids, IA 52403-3304

Directions: From US 151 (1st Ave.) turn left on 18th St. SE.
Turn right on Mt. Vernon Road.

Ghost Lore

Every day thousands of people visit cemeteries. Usually they go in, pay their respects to the deceased, and then continue on with their day. However, the same cannot be said for Oak Hill Cemetery. If you go to this cemetery at night, you may not be able to leave.

The graveyard is haunted by a young woman who makes her presence known by ensnaring those brave enough to pass through at night.

9

- The ghost of a young Czech woman will grant your wish.

- Disrespectful visitors to Tillie's grave will encounter bad luck.

History

1853 – Reference books show that the land was first considered for a cemetery.

1854 – The cemetery was established. It began as a private for-profit cemetery.

1906 – The front gate was built through a gift from Lawson Daniels, the President of Oak Hill Cemetery.

1918 – The Turner Funeral Home opened.

1918 – The limestone receiving vault was last used.

1968 – The cemetery was turned into a not-for-profit cemetery.

1970s – The fence around Tillie's grave was removed.

Investigation

The Oak Hill Cemetery is filled with much history and intrigue.

At the front of the cemetery sat the receiving vault. The vault was used for those who had a loved one pass away but could not bury them immediately. Instead of keeping the body at the home while the details of the funeral were worked out, the family would store the body at the vault. The Oak Hill vault was no longer needed with the opening of the Turner Funeral Home that provided a place to store the body.

The cemetery has many unique characters buried inside. Several people buried in the cemetery have birth dates in the 1700s. The dentist who posed for Iowa's Grant Wood's *American Gothic* painting is buried in the cemetery. A victim from the 1912 Titanic sinking also claims Oak Hill Cemetery as his final resting place.

While most believe Tillie's grave is in Oak Hill Cemetery, some investigators believe that Tillie is buried in a neighboring cemetery.

There is much speculation surrounding the history of Tillie. What is agreed upon is that Tillie was a young Czech woman who lived in Cedar Rapids during the 1800s. From this point, the stories vary.

There is a Tillie who is buried in the graveyard. However, the record of where her plot is has been lost. We spoke with a cemetery employee who had been working at the graveyard for over ten years. He told us that no one knows where Tillie is actually buried. Most employees believe that Tillie's now unmarked grave is located in a small open area.

Witnesses report seeing a mysterious ghostly woman walking the old cemetery grounds. People often notice the ghost because she is said to be holding a small flickering candle in her hand.

One of the more popular legends of Tillie states that she was a practicing witch in Cedar Rapids. The residents were scared of her and

11

her occult practices. The town decided that the safest way to deal with her was to stone her to death. The town was fearful that Tillie would come back to take her revenge on them so they erected a wrought-iron fence around her grave in order to prevent Tillie from coming back. The grave marker had an inscription written in Czech that only fueled the rumors of Tillie's ghostly return.

Employees did confirm that years ago the grave was surrounded by an iron gate. However, the gate acted as a beacon for curious visitors, vandals, and cult members performing rituals at the site. This eventually led to the gate being removed from the grave. The removal of the gate is said to have freed the spirit of Tillie, causing her to roam the cemetery.

We spoke with an employee that believed Tillie was actually stoned to death in Green Square Park in Cedar Rapids.

Another variation is that Tillie was one of the first pioneer land owners of the area where the cemetery now sits. Tillie lived in her small house for many years as the cemetery started to rise up

around her. When she passed away, she was buried in a mausoleum within the cemetery. Beware—it is said that if you peek into Tillie's mausoleum, her ghostly hand will reach out and grab you, pulling you in to her domain where you will be forced to keep her company for eternity.

Still another story tells of Tillie living a long and poor life in Cedar Rapids. She passed away with no money or possessions and was buried in the Potter's Field section of the cemetery. This story may be the most accurate as Tillie was a very common name in Cedar Rapids, especially among the Czech residents.

Tillie also seems to have supernatural powers. If you are lucky enough to find Tillie's unknown grave you be rewarded for your vigilance with 30 days of good luck. However if you decide to be disrespectful while touring the graveyard you will be cursed with 30 days of bad luck for your indiscretion.

Cresco Theatre

Location: Cresco, Howard County, Iowa
Address: 115 Second Avenue West, Cresco, IA 52136-1517
Phone: (563) 547-4292
Toll-free: 1-800-846-7469
Seats: 275
National Register of Historic Places: #81000245

Ghost Lore

Many of Iowa's original grand old opera houses have long since been demolished; however, the opera house in Cresco is still standing and in use to this day. Some people believe that more than just the building has survived; they believe the spirits of dead performers and patrons continue to live on in the old theatre.

- Ghosts tamper with the projector and lighting equipment.

- Shadowy figures have been seen in the basement.

- Apparitions dressed as old-time vaudevillian performers have been seen.

- Phantom theatregoers have been spotted sitting in the theatre, but disappear when approached.

History

1914 – The Cresco Opera House was built by the community.

1915 – February 18. The Opera House officially opened. It featured traveling music shows, live performances, vaudeville, and moving pictures.

1920s to 1970s – Later it had a number of private owners and eventually fell into disrepair.

1978 – It was repurchased by the community and renovated to its original grandeur. The basement, known as Chaplin Hall, was remodeled to be used for meetings and meals.

1981 – Added to the National Register of Historic Places.

Today – It is fully restored. Serves as a movie theatre. The Cresco Community Theatre puts on live performances.

Investigation

Although there has been significant remodeling to the three-story structure, it still houses the original brick-lined projection booth in the back of the balcony. In addition, the stage still has working footlights from its vaudeville days.

Some of the former employees report that most of the haunting activity begin during the 1978 renovation.

Workers have had the alarming experience of seeing a mysterious, lone figure sitting in the empty, darkened theatre, as if waiting for a performance. When the person is approached, they vanish into thin air.

Others report hearing voices and strange sounds in the theatre when the building is supposedly empty.

There have been sightings of apparitions on or near the stage area. Most often, these phantoms are described as being dressed as vaudevillian performers from the early 1900s.

Porter House

Location: Decorah, Winneshiek County, Iowa
Official Name: The Porter House Museum
Address: 401 West Broadway Street, Decorah, IA 52101-1741
Mailing Address: P.O. Box 115, Decorah, IA 52101-0115
Phone: (563) 382-8465
Website: www.porterhousemuseum.com

Ghost Lore

Do you remember the theme to *The Addams Family*?

> They're creepy and they're kooky,
> Mysterious and spooky,
> They're all together ooky,
> The Addams Family.

Their house is a museum
Where people come to see 'em
They really are a scream
The Addams Family.

(Neat)
(Sweet)
(Petite)

So get a witches shawl on
A broomstick you can crawl on
We're gonna pay a call on
The Addams Family.

That theme could easily apply to the Porter House in Decorah. This older, Victorian mansion, with its looming tower, really is a museum. Many people feel the house is mysterious and spooky, complete with an "ooky" stone wall that surrounds it. Others might describe it as creepy and kooky because of the ghosts that walk its halls.

- From outside, shadowy figures have been seen standing at the window in the tower.

- Prankster ghosts inhabit the home and like to hide objects, then return them to unexpected locations.

- Apparitions, believed to be Mr. and Mrs. Porter have been seen on the staircase, up in the tower, and down in the basement.

- Phantom butterflies have been seen to fly by, but when the rooms are thoroughly searched, nothing is found.

History

1867 – This stately Italianate-style estate was built by D.B. Ellsworth.

1879 – February 16. Adelbert "Bert" Field Porter was born and raised by his grandparents, Samuel and Jamson Field.

1880 – Grace, daughter of Frank and Emma Young, was born.

1898 – The Youngs purchased the Ellsworth house.

1904 – Grace Young, fell in love with Bert Porter, who lived across the street. In June they were married in the music parlor of Grace's house.

1939-1945 – Porter built the stone wall around his house.

1964 – Grace died at age 84.

1968 – March. Bert died at age 89. After his death, the house was donated to the Winneshiek County Historical Society and opened as a museum. It houses a collection of butterflies, moths, insects, and rocks.

Investigation

Bert Porter was a naturalist who traveled the world collecting specimens of rare and exotic butterflies and insects. He was also an artist who created unusual forms of art using some of the moths and butterflies he had collected. His travel gear and many of the items he collected are on display in the museum.

The house is surrounded by a stone wall designed by Porter and built with unusual stones he had collected from around Iowa and other parts of the United States. It also includes gems, fossils, and petrified wood.

Grace Porter was also a talented artist who painted chinaware. Her work is on display in the dining room.

Despite their world travels, the Porters were very attached to their home and enjoyed being there, so it is not surprising their spirits would continue to inhabit the beautiful house.

Curators have reported the playful nature of the spirits. Objects will disappear, then turn up days later in unexpected places.

Visitors report seeing mysterious figures standing at the window after the museum has closed. Apparitions believed to be Bert and Grace have been seen in the house, mostly on the staircase and in the tower. Shadowy figures have been seen in the basement and sometimes outside behind the stone wall.

Most curious of all are the phantom butterflies. Perhaps they are a sign from the Porters to assure people that they are still at home and keeping watch over their collections.

So, the next time you're in Decorah, get a witches shawl on and a broomstick you can crawl on. We recommend you pay a call on the Porter family.

Ham House Phantom Pirate

Location: Dubuque, Dubuque County, Iowa
Official Name: Mathias Ham House Historic Site
Address: 2241 Lincoln Avenue, Dubuque, IA 52001-1424
Mailing Address: P.O. Box 266, Dubuque, IA 52004-0266
Phone: (563) 583-2812

Directions: Located at the entrance to Eagle Point Park.

Ghost Lore

Mathias Ham was one of the early settlers in Dubuque. He was a successful entrepreneur who built a mansion on top of a hill so he could sit up in his tower and watch over his fleet of ships on the Mississippi River. One day he spied his ships being harassed by river pirates. He alerted the authorities, and the pirates were arrested, but they swore they would one day get revenge on Ham.

Years later, Ham's daughter Sarah was the last surviving member of the family. She eventually inherited the family fortune and the Ham House, where she lived alone. Sarah told neighbors she was having problems with prowlers late at night, and they suggested she put a light in her window if she ever needed help. A couple nights later, she was in her room on the third floor reading in bed when she again heard the intruder. She put a lamp in her window, locked her bedroom door and grabbed a loaded gun. She heard footsteps come up the stairs and stop outside her door. When she called out, nobody answered, so she shot through the door twice. The neighbors heard the gunshots and saw the light in her window. They rushed over to her house and found a trail of blood leading from her bedroom door down to the river where they discovered the dead body of the pirate captain who had recently been released from prison and apparently had returned to seek the revenge he had promised.

Today the mansion is believed to be haunted by several ghosts, including the spirit of the pirate and the spirit of Mathias Ham.

Supposedly the ghost of the pirate is still searching for Sarah and looking for revenge. The ghost of Mathias Ham is protecting his beloved home and still watching over the river from his tower.

- The tower is haunted by a man who hanged himself there in the early 1900s.

- The staircase and third floor is haunted by the pirate.

- Cold spots and unexplained drafts.

- Strange noises. Sounds of footsteps, voices, crying, and screaming.

- Objects will mysteriously disappear and later reappear in different locations.

- Orbs of light will move through the house. The lights have also been seen outside on the property. Many believe it to be the lantern of the phantom pirate searching for Sarah to avenge his death.

- Uncomfortable feelings. The sense of an invisible presence that follows people around.

- Upstairs windows that were closed and locked are later found to be wide open. Doors will open and close on their own.

- Electrical problems. Lights that flicker, that will not work or that turn on by themselves after the museum is closed. On one occasion a curator, alone in the museum, was closing up for the day. She was unscrewing a fuse to shut off the lights to the front rooms when suddenly she heard organ music begin to play. She screwed the fuse back in, and the music instantly stopped. There is an organ in the mansion, but it is nonfunctional. The curator believed this was the ghost's way of telling her he did not want to be in the dark that night. She left the lights on, locked up, and left as quickly as she could.

History

1805 – April 12. Mathias Ham was born in Knox County, Tennessee.

1833 – After the treaty known as the Black Hawk Purchase pushed the Native Americans westward, non-Indian settlers began moving into the Iowa Territory. Ham settled in Dubuque that year and eventually made a huge fortune as a cabbage planter. He became known as the "Sauerkraut King."

1837 – While visiting Kentucky he married his first wife Zerelda Marklin.

1839 – Mathias built a stone house in Dubuque where he lived with his wife. They had six children together: Felly, Lewisan, Sidney, Thomas Benton, Zerilda Jane, and Sarah Etherington (b. 1855).

1856 – Zerelda died at age 43.

1856 to 1857 – Ham built a sumptuous, 23-room, limestone mansion. The home's Italianate architecture was designed by John F. Rague. A spiral staircase with 25 steps extended from the third floor to the eight-sided cupola where Ham was able to view the surrounding area.

1857 – September 9. Mathias married his second wife, Margaret Mclean. They later had two children: Mathias (b. 1862) and Maggie May (b. 1864). During the financial crash of 1857, Ham lost most of his money.

1874 – August. Margaret died.

1889 – March 8. Mathias died. His daughter Sarah, the last surviving member of the family, inherited the house.

1912 – Sarah no longer had any credit left to borrow money and was forced to sell the Ham House to the city for $10,000.

1921 – May 15. Sarah Ham died.

1964 – The Dubuque County Historical Society converted the house into a museum.

Investigation

The newspapers referred to Sarah Ham as one of the "reigning belles of the upper Mississippi River" in the 1870s and early 1880s. When she was 17, she fell in love with 30-year-old George A. Potter. Three years later the two of them began a sexual liaison that was to last 30 years. Initially she thought he was single. Later she discovered he had a wife and family back in Wisconsin. He told her his wife refused to grant him a divorce, but promised Sarah he would marry her after his wife died. The two of them were secretly engaged, but unhappy because they couldn't marry. Sarah was young and beautiful. She refused proposals of marriage from a number of prominent suitors because she was waiting for Potter to marry her. Over the years they made several trips out East and abroad together. While she lived in Iowa and he lived in Wisconsin, he wrote to her every day—sometimes two and three times a day for almost 30 years.

In Wisconsin, Potter owned a department store and creamery in Pittsville and a lumber business in Neenah. Sarah was the last surviving member of her family and inherited the house in 1889. She gave Potter the title to her house and loaned him $15,000 which he invested and turned into an immense fortune. Although he was a millionaire, he never paid her back, and she eventually lost her house. In 1901, Potter's wife died, but he never married Sarah as promised.

In 1903, Sarah caused a sensation in Dubuque when she filed a damage suit for breach of promise against Potter. She wanted $100,000. Potter in his answer to the petition, denied he ever promised to marry her, claimed she was a prostitute, and accused her of blackmail.

The newspaper described it as "one of the most sensational love affairs that ever got into court." The trial was held in 1904 in Duluth, Minnesota, where Potter was living at the time. Sarah transported a large trunk from Dubuque to Duluth. It contained over 1000 love letters that Potter had written to her over the years. Sarah's attorney read the letters in court. The newspapers described the letters as "teeming with all the terms of fond endearment of which the English language is capable." One paper described the letters as "hot stuff." They contained references to Potter's business affairs, "but by far the greater part was devoted to love-making." Frequently, Sarah covered her face with her gloved hands during the reading of some of the more intimate details, while curious spectators in the back of the courtroom snickered. The headline read, "LOVE LETTERS AMUSE SPECTATORS IN COURT: Attorneys for Miss Ham Read Millionaire Potter's Epistles."

She accused him of drugging her; he accused her of being an immoral woman. She claimed they were engaged; he claimed she was his mistress. She told the court he was locked up in an insane asylum from 1891 to 1897; he said it was her fault, because of the shock of discovering she had cheated on him. She accused him of being a con artist; he claimed the Ham House was used as a house of prostitution by the Ham girls and that they also worked as prostitutes elsewhere. He maintained he rescued her from a life of prostitution. The papers called it "the most sensational trial ever heard in the northwest."

After a week-long trial, the jury deliberated 55 minutes, then awarded Sarah $20,000. The headline splashed across the front page read, "RICH MAN WHO MADE LOVE MUST PAY $20,000 FOR HIS FUN." Although he was supposedly a millionaire, Potter claimed to be insolvent and unable to pay the judgment. The following year he appealed, but his appeal was refused by the district court.

Despite all the media coverage Sarah received in her lifetime, there was never any mention of the alleged incident with the pirate. Because the newspapers were always on the lookout for a sensational story, it is difficult to believe they would have ignored this one. Moreover, if Sarah had shot and killed a man, Potter most certainly would have mentioned it in court during his attempt to malign her.

Our investigation also failed to find any evidence of a suicide in the tower. Again, it is not believable that the newspapers would overlook a story such as this, considering the fact that the Ham family was so prominent in Dubuque.

Although the stories of the pirate and the suicide are suspect, the stories of the haunting activity in the house are apparently true. Museum employees and visitors to the house continue to report strange haunting activity. Perhaps it is the brokenhearted ghost of the spinster Sarah, still waiting for someone to marry her.

Grand Opera House

Location: Dubuque, Dubuque County, Iowa
Address: The Grand Opera House, 135 West Eighth Street,
Dubuque, IA 52001-6810
Mailing Address: The Grand Opera House, P.O. Box 632
Dubuque, IA 52004-0632
Business Office Phone: (563) 588-4356
Box Office Phone: (563) 588-1305
Fax: (563) 588-3497
Email: boxoffice@thegrandoperahouse.com
Website: www.thegrandoperahouse.com

Ghost Lore

"Grand" certainly is a fitting name for this lavish structure. The
Grand Opera House is the oldest theater in Dubuque and at one
time was the city's largest theatre. Done in the Richardsonian
architectural style, the original facade consists of St. Louis brick

facing with Bayfield red sandstone trim.

Do the ghosts of some of the early theatergoers still sit in the auditorium late at night and wait for the curtains to rise? Do the spirits of some of the early performers, such as Henry Fonda, still grace the stage as phantom actors? Some people think so.

- Employees hear strange noises, sounds of footsteps, and voices late at night.

- Ghosts play pranks. Objects disappear and later reappear elsewhere.

- Electrical problems with lighting and sound equipment.

- Ghosts of two women seen sitting in the auditorium vanish when approached.

History

1889 – The Grand Opera House Company was established by William Lester Bradley, Sr. and 50 private citizens.

1889 to 1890 – The Grand Theatre was built at a cost of $65,000. It had a seating capacity of 1,100 and a huge stage that measured 42 feet from front to back. The stage was so massive that during a production of *Ben Hur* it featured chariots and live horses and elephants. The theatre hosted legendary stars such as George M. Cohan (1878-1942), Sarah Bernhardt (1844-1923), Lillian Russell (1860-1922), Ethel Barrymore (1879-1959), and Henry Fonda (1905-1982).

1915 – The Grand began occasionally showing moving pictures, and the movies earned three times more profit than live theatre.

1928 – Live theatre ceased.

1930 – The second balcony was removed, reducing the seating capacity from 1100 to 644. It was converted into a movie house with a big screen and known as "The Grand."

1986 – The Barn Community Theatre purchased the building, renovated it, and started doing live theatre again. They have produced comedies, dramas, musicals, children's shows and many other attractions.

Investigation

Does the ghost of Henry Fonda haunt this theatre? In his later years, Fonda reminisced of his fond memories of having played *Hamlet* at the Grand Theatre in 1923. Performing here was a cherished experience for him, so it is certainly possible that he visits the theatre.

Employees did confirm the reports of strange sounds and tamperings with the electronic equipment. Former ushers did talk about the time when they inspected what should have been an empty auditorium, only to find two older women sitting together in the front row as if waiting for a performance. When the ushers approached them, the woman either could not be found or they simply vanished while the ushers stood dumbfounded.

Lover's Leap

Location: Elkader, Clayton County, Iowa

Directions: From Hwy 56 in Elkader, turn on Bridge St. Take the bridge across the Turkey River. Turn left on High St. N.E. Turn left on Sandlot Rd. The Turkey River will be on the left and some county office buildings will be on the right. Turn right on the narrow, unpaved driveway just past these buildings. At the end of the driveway are more county-owned buildings. A dirt trail begins here and leads up a steep embankment to the top of the hill, terminating at the rock outcropping known as Lover's Leap.

WARNING: The climb to the top is strenuous and dangerous. There are no stairs, handrails, or safety fences. It is not recommended for pregnant woman, small children, the elderly, or people with health issues. It is especially not a safe place to be after dark or while intoxicated.

DISCLAIMER: We recommend that people observe Lover's

Leap only from below on Sandlot Rd. Those who decide to climb to the top do so at their own risk and against our advice. We are not responsible for any personal injuries or death that may result.

Ghost Lore

A young Indian woman named White Cloud fell in love with a white settler, but her tribe disapproved of the relationship. One day, some warriors from her tribe ambushed her lover and left him for dead. White Cloud was told he had been killed, and she was so brokenhearted she committed suicide by jumping from a nearby cliff. Unknown to her, her beloved had survived the attack. Days later, he found her body and buried her in an unmarked grave on

top of the place she had jumped from. Since that time, the bluff has been known as Lover's Leap.

People have seen the apparition of the beautiful, young Indian woman standing at the edge of the precipice.

History

1673 – French explorers came through this area and discovered lead mines. At that time, the region was home to about 17 different Indian tribes; however, years later, most sold their land to the Federal government and moved west. The two largest tribes, the Sauk (Sac) and Fox (Mesquakie), remained. For centuries the Indians had been mining lead for utilitarian and ornamental objects.

1786 – Julien Dubuque (1762-1810), a French miner, purchased land from the Fox Indians and set up a trading and mining outpost in the area that would one day be the city of Dubuque, Iowa. He is considered to be Iowa's first European settler. Over a period of 22 years, he made a huge fortune mining lead. It is widely believed he

was married to Petosa, the daughter of Fox Chief Peosta.

1810 – Dubuque died after a prolonged illness–possibly lead poisoning. Creditors and land speculators from St. Louis tried to claim the mines, but they were driven out by the Fox who burned all of Dubuque's buildings.

1829 – James L. Langworthy (1800-1865), a lead miner from Galena, Illinois, heard about the lead mines on the western side of the Mississippi and decided to investigate. He became friends with the Fox and Sauk and asked their permission to mine but was refused. They did, however, allow him to explore the region. He hired two young Indians as guides, and for three weeks traveled the region between the Maquoketa and Turkey Rivers searching for lead mines. Then he returned to Galena.

1830 – Langworthy once again crossed the Mississippi. This time with his brother Lucius H. Langworthy (1807-1865). Lucius is famous for having given the name "Iowa" to the territory. The brothers engaged in lead mining in the old Dubuque mines.

Under treaty, this was still Indian territory, and the brothers were there illegally. Future US President Col. Zachary Taylor and future President of the Confederacy Jefferson Davis were stationed at Fort Crawford, and it was their job to keep the white settlers out of the Iowa region. They sent an officer who gave the brothers 10 days to stop mining and to return to the eastern bank of the Mississippi. The Langworthys refused to move. Col. Taylor dispatched troops and they forced the men out. It was necessary to station troops in Dubuque to keep white settlers out.

1831 – The Corn Treaty. The Federal government claimed ownership of what is today Illinois, and the Indians on the eastern side of the Mississippi River were forced to move across the river into what is today Iowa and to live in assigned areas. The Sioux were given northern Iowa; the Sauk and Fox were assigned the southern land.

1832 – The Black Hawk War. Ma-ka-tai-me-she-kia-kiak, better known as Chief Black Hawk (1767-1838), was a Sauk leader who resisted the move. The Indian prophet Waubeshiek, known as White Cloud (1794–1841), was a friend and advisor to Black Hawk. His advice to Black Hawk was that if the Sauk were attacked by US forces, not only would the British come to their rescue, but so would the Winnebago, Potawatomi, Chippewa, and Ottawa tribes. This advice proved to be wrong.

The Illinois militia promptly forced Black Hawk out and pursued him and his people for three months through northern Illinois and Wisconsin. James L. Langworthy served as a scout and later a captain during the war. Future President Abraham Lincoln also enlisted and served as a captain. In what became known as the Bad Axe Massacre, the soldiers killed dozens of the Sauk, including women, children and the elderly as they were attempting to cross the Mississippi River into Iowa. Black Hawk was captured near Wisconsin Dells.

In September, as a punishment against Black Hawk, the government wrote up the Black Hawk Treaty which took an additional strip of land 50 miles wide on the west shore of the Mississippi. It stretched from the Missouri border to what would later be Fayette and Clayton counties in northeastern Iowa. The troops that were stationed in Dubuque to protect the Indians were now ordered to push them west.

Before the treaty was ratified, the eastern shore of the Mississippi was lined with white settlers eager to get across to grab up the land. Some of them illegally ventured in early to explore the territory and to find the best locations, but they did so at the peril of their own lives. They were quickly driven out by US troops and by the Indians.

After the Indians had been removed, the Langworthy brothers returned to Dubuque and settled once again. Because the Black Hawk Treaty had not officially gone into effect, the US troops forced them out, tore down their cabins, and burned their wagons and property. The brothers retreated to an island on the Mississippi with 300,000 lbs of lead. They lived in a makeshift cabin and waited for the treaty to be ratified.

1833 – The Black Hawk Treaty. June 1. After the treaty was ratified, the Langworthy brothers moved back to Dubuque and resumed their mining business which made them a huge profit. With their wealth and influence they built the city of Dubuque.

Thousands of people moved into the area of Clayton and Dubuque counties. People crossing the Mississippi from Cassville, Wisconsin, founded Millville, which is considered to be the first white settlement in Iowa.

1836 – Elisha Boardman and Horace Bronson followed the Turkey River northwest to the Pony Hollow area. They were the first white settlers there and founded the town of Elkader. Boardman established the first farm and together with other early settlers built the first schoolhouse.

1846 – Elkader was officially platted. It was laid out by Timothy Davis, John Thompson and Chester Sage. Elkader was named after Abdel-Kader, a young Algerian hero who led his people in a resistance to French colonialism between 1830 and 1847.

1880 – Elkader became the county seat.

Investigation

Another version of the legend has it that one of the lead miners fell in love with an Indian chief's daughter. When the two of them got caught stealing lead, they were knocked unconscious. It is unclear if they were attacked by members of her tribe or by other miners. When the young woman regained consciousness, she assumed her lover was dead and threw herself off the cliff. When he came to and found her dead body, he also took his life by jumping from the same cliff.

The book, *Old Elkader Facts and Food* (published by the Elkader Historical Society in 1976), provides a third version of the legend and attempts to fill in some of the blanks by adding names, dates, and places:

> Around 1831, the Millville family lived above Dubuque. Their son, Lou, not only found companionship among neighboring Indians, he was particularly friendly with Chief Grey Eagle and his beautiful daughter, White Cloud.
>
> Millville knew the Indians had a lead mine some distance from Dubuque. Against the advice of White Cloud, Lou followed two braves into the wilderness to learn the secret of the mines. Far up the Turkey River, he was discovered and captured by the Indians. At dawn, the following morning, Lou was ordered to leap from the cliff into the water far below. As he stood poised to jump, he instead leaped backward to attack his captors. Before he lost consciousness from tomahawk blows Lou managed to throw his assailants over the cliff. When Millville recovered, he found White Cloud's moccasins beside him.
>
> Fearing for his safety, White Cloud had followed Millville in her canoe. She had discovered him lying on the cliff and thinking him dead, removed her moccasins and leaped over the cliff. Millville found the dying White Cloud on the rocks near the water's edge. He later buried her on the cliff from which she had jumped. Legend says the faithful lover made a yearly pilgrimage to the grave of White Cloud located on what is now known as Lover's Leap.

After attempting to verify the details of this story, we found some aspects of it to be questionable.

First, there is a problem with the date. Although there may have been white miners illegally living in this territory in 1831, no white families settled in the Dubuque area until 1833, and they did not reach the Elkader area until 1836. By then the Indians had been pushed to the west.

Second, there is a problem with the names. We were unable to find any record of a Lou Millville. We did find a Louis Miller who lived in Dubuque, but he moved there in 1850 (long after the Indians were pushed west), was married to a white woman, had nine children, and was a hotel proprietor, not a miner. He hardly fits the bill.

When we attempted to expand our search for other members of the Millville family, we were unable to locate the surname "Millville" anywhere in Iowa—or in the United States for that matter. We did notice the town of Millville just 30 miles from Elkader. However, it was named for the mill the village used to have; not for a family of that name. This made us suspicious.

Looking at a map of Iowa and the surrounding states, we saw White Cloud Township, 300 miles to the southwest, in Mills County, Iowa (notice the similarity between Mills and Millville). There was also White Cloud, Kansas, 400 miles to the southwest, and White Cloud, Missouri, 450 miles to the south. In addition, we found a Grey Eagle, Minnesota, 300 miles to the northwest. Could somebody have come up with the names in the legend by looking at a map? Possibly.

In our historical research for White Cloud, we were unable to find any information on an Indian woman with that name. There was White Cloud the prophet who was the friend and advisor to Chief Black Hawk. We also found a Chief Louis White Cloud (1869-1947) who was the head of the Iowa Indian Tribe. Could somebody have derived the names "Lou" and "White Cloud" from his name and applied them to this story? Possibly.

Finally, we could find no record of a Chief Grey Eagle amongst the Fox, Sauk, or any other tribe in Iowa. We did, however, find a story about a Chief Grey Eagle in Tallulah Falls, Georgia—a thousand miles from Elkader—and there is an interesting legend about him. It seems his only daughter Tallulah fell in love with a white man. When the members of her tribe bound him hand and foot and cast him off a cliff, Tallulah came running from behind and jumped to her death. Since that time the cliff has been known as "Lover's Leap."

What is even more interesting is that we found several other Lover's Leaps throughout the Midwest.

Lansing, Iowa. Just 50 miles northeast of Elkader, there is another Lover's Leap, with a legend of a young Indian girl who promised to marry the bravest of her two suitors. To prove his courage, one of the young men leaped off a cliff to his death; the other, not wanting to appear cowardly, followed, leaving the young woman doubly forlorn.

Alton, Illinois. Located 400 miles south, is yet another Lover's Leap. The story is told of a young Indian girl, Laughing Water, who fell in love with Black Otter. Her father disapproved of Black Otter and shot an arrow at him. He only intended to wing him, but missed and accidentally killed his daughter. Thereupon the grief-stricken Black Otter picked up her lifeless body into his arms and jumped off a cliff.

Viroqua, Wisconsin. This town, about 70 miles northeast of Elkader, has the Legend of the Princess. In one variation of the legend, it is said that Viroqua was the daughter of Chief Black Hawk. During the Black Hawk War of 1832, she was separated from her tribe as they were chased by the military. It is said she hid in a cave near what is today the town of Viroqua. After a few days she thought it was safe to come out, but was spotted and chased by the soldiers. She rode her horse to the edge of some high rocks, but was cornered. She ended her life by leaping off the cliff.

Maiden Rock, Wisconsin. Located on the mighty Mississippi about 165 miles to the north of Elkader, this town is named after the nearby Maiden Rock Cliff that overlooks the river. In the Princess Winona legend, the daughter of Dakota Indian Chief Red Wing (for whom the town of Red Wing, Minnesota is named) fell in love with a boy who was a member of the rival Chippewa tribe. When her father had her boyfriend killed by warriors from the Dakota tribe, she took her life by leaping from a cliff.

In another version of the story, she jumped off the cliff and accidentally landed on her parents below, killed both. Afterwards, the girl ran off with her boyfriend, and they lived happily every after.

Hannibal, Missouri. Further down the Mississippi, in Mark Twain's hometown, located 250 miles south of Elkader, is another outcrop of rock on the river known as "lover's leap." Legend has it that many years ago an Indian girl living on the Hannibal side of the river fell in love with an Indian boy on the Illinois side. Their tribes were at war with each other so they kept their relationship a secret. One day, during a clandestine rendezvous atop a rocky precipice, they were surrounded by the warriors from her tribe. The young lovers embraced each other and leaped to their death.

So what do we make of all these stories? Are they simply the invention of romantics? Possibly. Mark Twain was skeptical of the veracity of these tales. In *Life on the Mississippi*, he wrote: "There are fifty Lover's Leaps along the Mississippi from whose summit disappointed Indian girls have jumped."

Most debunkers reject these stories out of hand because of the similarities, but it could easily be countered that leaping from a cliff was probably a common method of suicide back in the time when there were no high bridges or tall buildings to jump from.

Although we can neither prove nor disprove that someone committed suicide off Lover's Leap in Elkader, we do know people continue to report seeing the phantom figure of a young Indian girl standing precariously close to the edge.

The Barefoot Outlaws

Location: Independence, Buchanan County, Iowa
Official Name: Buchanan County Court House
Address: 210 Fifth Avenue Northeast, Independence, IA 50644-11959
Mailing Address: P.O. Box 259, Independence, IA 50644-0259
Phone: (319) 334-2196
Fax: (319) 334-7455

Ghost Lore

We have investigated cases of ghosts missing their heads or their faces or even their legs, but this is the first case we've come upon where the ghosts are noted for missing their footwear. The Buchanan County Court House is said to be haunted by phantoms who wear no shoes.

- The sounds of bare feet walking down empty corridors.

- Heavy doors mysteriously opening and closing on their own.

- Apparitions of a barefooted man with a noose tied around his neck. Sometimes seen standing in a jail cell. Other times seen hanging from the ceiling.

History

1858 – Isaac "Ike" Barber was born in Fayette, Iowa.

1860 – William "Bill" Barber was born in Fayette, Iowa.

1862 to 1863 – Their father, Lawrence E. Barber, served in Company K of the Iowa Regiment during the Civil War. He was discharged due to disability and died shortly afterwards. The boys were placed in the Soldier's Orphans Home at Cedar Falls.

1870 – The old jail and sheriff's house were built in Independence at a cost of $18,828.00.

1878 – Ike, 20, married Hattie Slauter and later had two sons (Fred and George). Bill, 18, married her sister Alice Slauter and later had three children: Gertrude (Gurtie) and William (Willie) and another son.

1882 – Ike and Bill shot and killed a deputy sheriff.

1883 – The brothers were captured and lynched.

Investigation

We spoke with several old-timers who had vague memories of hearing stories about a hanging that occurred many years ago. It was not known if the hanging was the result of an execution, a suicide, or a lynching. They did recall that the hanging was not an instant death with the snapping of a neck; but, rather, was a slow

strangulation. They also knew that bare feet were somehow significant, but they could not remember why.

The details were just a little too hazy, and we suspected we were
dealing with nothing more than folklore, but after several days of
research, we finally uncovered the facts of the case.

1882. The Barber brothers, Ike and Bill, worked for a farmer who
cheated them out of their wages, so they appropriated one of his
horses and sold it for cash. On September 7th, Deputy Sheriff

Isaac "Ike" Barber

Bremer County Historical Society

Marion Shepherd (also spelled Shephard, Shepard, Sheppard) came to arrest them for horse theft. He ordered them to surrender, then pulled his revolver and fired, grazing Bill in the head. In self-defense, Ike drew his gun and killed the sheriff. The brothers had never intended to be outlaws, but now they were concerned that people would view them as being another feared and hated gang like their contemporaries, the James brothers (Frank and Jesse) and the Younger brothers (Cole, Jim, John, and Bob). Later one newspaper even referred to them as the "rival of the James Gang."

A search party was organized by the authorities, but members of the posse would retreat in fear each time they came face-to-face with the brothers.

Bremer County Historical Society

Ike lynched

45

The Barber brothers traveled almost 500 miles southwest to Kansas and hid out in Clay County where they picked corn for a farmer and later operated a ferry on the Republican River.

Monday, May 28, 1883. Nine months had passed, and the brothers missed their friends and family back in Iowa. Because people who had encountered them earlier were afraid of them, they assumed it would be safe to return. They believed they had only wounded the deputy sheriff and had no knowledge they were wanted for his murder and they were also being blamed for every crime

Bremer County Historical Society

William "Bill" Barber

in the Midwest that could not be laid on the Jesse James gang, including a triple homicide in Illinois. Illinois was offering a $5,000 reward and Iowa was offering a $1,000 for the capture of the Barber brothers. They purchased train tickets and traveled to Independence. From there, they traveled to West Union where they were originally from.

They discovered their mother had moved to the town of Glendive in the Montana Territory just six week earlier, so after some discussion the brothers agreed they should leave the country permanently and go live with her. They purchased train tickets for Montana Territory, but decided to first visit their six sisters.

Bremer County Historical Society

Bill lynched

47

As they were entering one of the houses to visit a sister, a young boy recognized them and alerted the local authorities, and the brothers made a hasty getaway.

Sunday.   June 3, 1883. The brothers hid in the Pinhook Schoolhouse three miles north of Sumner, but were spotted by a local resident. By 3:00 p.m., the town had been alerted.

A. H. Jarvis, the Bremer county deputy sheriff, organized a group of six to eight armed men and they headed for the schoolhouse. When they were near, Jarvis separated from the party and approached the school from the south. The brothers had left the schoolhouse and were bathing in the creek which runs through Wilson's grove. The posse found the brothers and began shooting at them. The fugitives attempted to escape by going south, but they encountered the sheriff. They shot him in the shoulder and managed to get away by wading across the creek, leaving behind their boots, coats, and ammunition. That was the last time they ever wore shoes. Thereafter, they were called the "shoeless thieves" or "barefoot outlaws."

By nightfall, a body of about 400 armed men were scouring the woods for the barefoot outlaws. That night the boys hid in Chaney Cook's barn on the banks of the Big Wapsie River.

Monday. June 4, 1883. Sheriff Fair of West Union arrived with 100 men. The sheriff of Black Hawk County departed from Waterloo to assist.

That night they were surrounded in a grove, but managed to escape during a heavy rain storm. They hid in E. Hallett's barn near Tripoli. They were hungry and went to the house to ask for food. Hallett answered the door, but when he lit his lantern, he saw their bare feet and knew who they were. They quickly ran off.

Tuesday.   June 5, 1883. In the morning they moved on and sought shelter in another barn six miles south of Tripoli This one was owned by a German farmer named Augustus Tegtmeir. That evening, when Tegtmeir's son Henry was milking the cows, the

Barber brothers crawled out of the hay and asked him for food. Henry saw their bare feet, but didn't let on that he knew who they were. He invited them into the house and had his mother prepare them a huge meal. Henry secretly instructed his mother to take her take her time, while he went out to the barn and alerted his father. Augustus gathered up the younger children and brought them to the neighbor's house.

The Barber brothers were eating the enormous supper prepared for them by Mrs. Tegtmeir. They had just asked for an extra loaf of bread when Augustus and three of his stalwart German neighbors burst into the room. The brothers grabbed their guns and started shooting. The Germans were unarmed except for an unloaded shotgun which one of them broke over Ike's head. Henry grabbed Bill by the throat and wrestled him to the floor. In the struggle, Bill nearly bit Henry's finger off. Ike leaped out a window and started shooting from outside, fatally wounding one of the neighbors, Henry Kasting, hitting him in the chest. Another neighbor, Henry Papa, slipped out through the cellar and grabbed Ike from behind. Ike turned and shot him, but despite the six-inch long and one-inch deep wound, the robust German would not loosen his hold. Mrs. Tegtmeir brought some rope from the barn, and they tied up the two outlaws.

Henry had to hold back his raging mother as she was hellbent on chopping off the heads of the two brothers. They sent for help and doctors arrived to tend their wounds, but Henry Kasting died three hours later. Deputy sheriffs Adair and Carstensen took the Barber brothers to Waverly and locked them up in the jail.

Wednesday. June 6, 1883. Word of the capture quickly spread. A lynch mob was being organized in Waverly and another was arriving from West Union. When Bill heard the news about the planned lynching, he was agitated and begged the sheriff to see his mother one last time before he died.

That evening, Sheriff Adair was concerned about the possible lynching and with his deputies took the brothers by wagon 22 miles to Janesville. From there, they were transported by the Illinois

Central passenger train to Independence and jailed there in the secure stone structure.

Later that night, the mob came to the Waverly jail demanding the Barber brothers. They were allowed to inspect the jail and were convinced the prisoners had been moved. They left disappointed. Many of them rode horse all night in every direction, determined to find where the brothers had been transported.

Thursday. June 7, 1883. Citizens of Independence learned the Barber brothers were in their jail and became concerned that the lynch mob would come to Independence.

A photographer convinced the sheriff to allow him to take several photos of the brothers in the jail. When it was suggested that a photo be sent to his wife, Ike broke down and "wept like a child."

News arrived from West Union that the lynch mob had learned of the brother's location and had set out for Independence. The citizens were concerned about an attack from the mob and asked the authorities for clubs to use as protection.

The authorities in Independence feared the mob would damage their new jail, so they sent the brothers back to Waverly knowing full well they would be lynched. The newspapers later described this as a disgrace to the state of Iowa and especially to the authorities at Independence. When the brothers were informed they were being moved back to Waverly, they pleaded with the authorities to either keep them in Independence or to transfer them to the state prison at Anamosa, but it was to no avail. When Sheriff Adair came for the prisoners, the authorities in Independence asked him what he would do in Waverly if the mob attempted to lynch the brothers. His reply was, "I can't help it if they knock me over with a paper bag."

Friday. June 8, 1883. 9:00 p.m. The mob of about 500 men went to the jail. Sheriff Adair refused to hand over the key. The mob broke into the blacksmith shop and stole two sledge hammers and a crowbar. They returned to the jail, and it took them half an hour to break in the heavy steel door. The first person to enter the jail cell was knocked out by one of the brothers before they were overpowered by the mob. A couple of men put hangman's ropes around their necks and dragged then down the stairs to a tree in the court yard. Sheriff Adair stuck his head out the window and asked them to not hang the brothers in town. The mob consented and took them outside the city limits to a cottonwood grove owned by Mike Murphy.

As a last request, Ike asked for a chew of tobacco. After some difficulty and a delay of five minutes, a plug was finally found for him. Then they were granted their last words. Ike confessed that he, not Bill, killed Shepherd and Kasting, but insisted he shot in self-defense. He also said they were not guilty of the other murders and robberies that were attributed to them. He requested that the crowd bury him so his family wouldn't have the expense.

When it was Bill's turn to talk, he said he had never killed anyone, and requested that his silk handkerchief and a gold pin be given to his little daughter. The leaders of the mob were hesitating about whether or not to lynch Bill, until an influential member of the community yelled, "Hang the son of a bitch!"

Shortly before midnight, they were brought to the trees where they were to be hanged. The crowd removed their hats to allow the brothers a final prayer.

Bill was hanged first. A rope was tied around his neck and he was raised about four feet from the ground. He did not struggle, but slowly strangled to death. It took him three minutes to die. Next, it was Ike's turn. After two and a half minutes he was unconscious and twelve minutes later he was dead. The necks of neither of them were broken; they were strangled, and both were dead before midnight. The crowd quietly dispersed, and the bodies were left hanging overnight.

Saturday. June 9, 1883. At noon, the coroner removed the bodies that still had bare feet and put them in coffins. They were buried that same day, and their families were notified. An examination of Bill's gun found it to be cheap and basically useless. It was probably true that he never killed anyone. That evening, Iowa's governor Buren R. Sherman visited Waverly and was distressed by the lynching.

Later, people were selling small pieces from the trees where the brothers had been hanged and were selling them for a quarter each as souvenirs. A week later a circus came to town and offered Mike Murphy $25 each for the trees. He ended up cutting them both down and disposing of them.

Many people believe that because Sheriff Adair stood by and allowed the lynching, he was cursed by the ghosts of the two brothers. Shortly thereafter, he went partially insane and had to be taken to the state hospital in Independence for treatment.

It is also said that Tripoli, the town where the brothers were apprehended, was cursed by them. Exactly one week after their capture, the town was devastated by a fierce tornado. It blew down trees and buildings. A large machinery warehouse was destroyed. Several people were injured. The newspapers described how businesses, homes, and small buildings were "blown to atoms."

It is speculated that the barefoot outlaws haunt the Buchanan County Court House jail because Independence is where they felt safe from the lynch mob, and they didn't want to leave this place.

Carlos O'Kelly's Mexican Cafe

Location: Marion, Linn County, Iowa
Address: 3320 Armar Drive, Marion, IA 52302-4701
Phone: (319) 373-1451

Directions: From Marion Street turn on Armar Drive.

Ghost Lore

At first glance, the Carlos O' Kelly's Restaurant looks to be just another place to get a meal. Located directly off the main road, it is surrounded by numerous other eating establishments for you to choose from. It comes complete with good atmosphere, great food, and friendly service. However, many believe that the restaurant offers something most other places do not, its very own ghost. You will have to ask your server about the ghost since it is not listed on the menu. But if you keep your eyes sharp you may just have your own unique dining experience.

- Poltergeist activity is often seen by the staff of the restaurant.

- Many restaurant appliances seem to work with a mind of their own.

History

It is believed that the site once housed a carnival.

1970 to 1980s – The restaurant was called Applegate's Landing.

1980s – Carlos O' Kelly's Restaurant opened.

Currently – Carlos O' Kelly's Restaurant is still operating in the building.

Investigation

A restaurant employee told us of a strange event that happened to her while she was closing up one evening. The woman was alone in the restaurant and had just finished cleaning her desk when she left the office to check on the phone that kept going on and off. She thought the phone problem was weird since it had never malfunctioned in the past, but passed it off as her nerves kicking in. When the woman returned to her office she was baffled when she discovered a cup of coffee had been mysteriously placed on her desk.

Several employees have been working during the evening when they see plates fly off the shelves for no apparent reason. Upon investigation the employees can never find a cause for the mysterious flying plates.

The plates are not the only items flying off the shelves, as employees report that cleaning supplies, cooking equipment, and other restaurant items also leap off the shelves on their own.

It appears that the restaurant appliances also exhibit weird behavior. Many employees report that the blenders normally used for making up margaritas turn on and off on their own.

Customers and employees have reported seeing the restaurant lights flickering and turn on and off without the aid of human intervention.

But beware—many of the employees are reluctant to speak about their personal experiences.

The Cursed Chair

Location: Marshalltown, Marshall County, Iowa

Directions: Follow Cemetery Street to the north and it will bring you right to the cemetery. The chair is located in the middle of the older back section (Section L).

Ghost Lore

Throughout this book you have read a lot of strange history, background, and local lore about each site. Some have been scary, some weird, and some very complicated. But for Riverside Cemetery, the ghost lore is simple—don't sit in the chair! It is said that the mysterious chair will cause death to anyone who dares to sit in it.

History

1863 – A movement to establish a cemetery was started by Louis DeLos and Dr. George Glick.

1863 – The Marshall Cemetery Association was formed.

1883 – The cemetery association was re-incorporated and the name of Riverside Cemetery was adopted.

1883 – The graves from Hartwell's Cemetery were reburied in Riverside Cemetery.

1890 – Samuel Rubee was the first employee of the cemetery. He was hired by the Marshall Cemetery Association.

1904 – Mr. H. E. Simkins operated a successful business as an undertaker and embalmer.

1946 – Superintendent Rubee passed away.

1946 – Clifford McMahon took his spot as the second superintendent.

1960 – James Hauser became the cemetery's superintendent.

1962 – Wallace Loft took the job of superintendent.

1991 – Mr. Loft retired.

Currently – The cemetery superintendent is Arlene Johnson.

Investigation

As old as Riverside Cemetery is, it was not the first cemetery in town. That distinction goes to Hartwell's Cemetery. All of the 58 graves in Hartwell's Cemetery were transferred to Riverside Cemetery. The Iowa Veterans Home now sits on the land that comprised Hartwell's Cemetery.

There is no inscription on the chair. However, the chair is located between two gravestones with the names Smith and Carlson. The chair may be part of one of those gravesites.

It is said that if you have the courage to sit on the chair you will die within one year of your risky action.

We spoke with several residents who had heard of the cursed chair and none of them had tempted fate by sitting in it.

We were unable to find any deaths associated with persons sitting in the chair.

This case is still pending.

Reece Park

Location: New Providence, Hardin County, Iowa

Directions: Go south on Co. Hwy. S57, then turn right on 310th Avenue.

Ghost Lore

Camping has always been a favorite weekend retreat from our daily lives. It allows us an opportunity to enjoy the great outdoors through fishing, hiking, or by simply staring at the wide-open night sky. Of course, the highlight for many campers is sitting around a warm crackling fire spinning or hearing a scary ghost story. However, those who choose to spend the night at the secluded Reece Park campground may end up with a few new ghost stories to tell.

- Several years ago a young girl committed suicide out in the country. The community was so distraught that a memorial park was then created for her.

- The ghost of the deceased girl is responsible for the haunting activity in the park.

- An eerie female scream echoes throughout the wooded park.

History

The Reece family has a long history in the area.

1755 – Abraham Reece was a young boy in Pennsylvania. Most of the Iowa Reeces trace their lineage back to him.

Abraham and Mary had 12 children: Daniel, Jemima, Eli, Levi, Abraham, Mary, Joel, Jesse, Keziah, Thomas, Sarah and John.

The area in Iowa was known as Reece Settlement.

1852 – A meeting was held near where the Honey Creek House now stands to establish a healthy religious being.

1852 – William Reece entered the first land deed near Honey Creek.

1852 – Four of the William children passed away.

1854 – The first school of the area was constructed near Honey Creek Cemetery. The teacher was James Talbott.

1895 – William Reece passed away.

Investigation

The title of the first landowner was a highly competitive event. William Reece did enter the first land deed for the area. However, he made a mistake on the numbering of the land. An unidentified man found this out and set out to Des Moines to claim the land for himself. William found out about this and decided that he had to made a fast trek to Des Moines to fix his mistake. After attending a religious meeting, Williams set off and walked non-stop though streams, prairie, and marshes. He was able to get to the office and reclaim his land. It is said that when he was walking out of the office, he encountered the man seeking his land.

The park, which was originally a pasture, was not named after a girl who was said to have committed suicide on the land. It was actually named after Linn Reece. We were unable to find any evidence of a suicide in the area.

Many of the Reeces are buried down the road at the Honey Creek Friends Cemetery.

Those who visit the park often report seeing a vaporous young woman floating around the park.

A loud female screaming noise of unknown origin has been heard passing through the trees.

Thirteen Steps Cemetery

Location: Palo, Linn County, Iowa
Official Name: Pleasant Ridge Cemetery

Directions: From Palo travel north on Palo Marsh Road (W36) for approximately four miles. The cemetery will be on your left. Turn left at the "no outlet" sign road.

Ghost Lore

The number 13 . . . is it just another number, or does it possess some supernatural significance? Why have people all over the world considered the number 13 unlucky for so long? The fear of the number 13 is called triskaidekaphobia. However, you do not need to have triskaidekaphobia to avoid the number 13, as many hotels do not have a room 13, elevators skip the 13th floor, and no one would want you to sit in row 13 on the airplane. But all this fear is just plain superstition right? Well those brave enough to walk up the 13 stairs to enter the Pleasant Ridge Cemetery believe there actually may be something to it.

- The cemetery is guarded by a ferocious phantom dog.

- Strange, colored lights have been reported dancing throughout the graveyard.

- A mysterious house has been spotted in the open area.

- During the daytime, only 12 steps are visible. To see all 13 steps, you must visit the cemetery at night.

History

Much of the history of this cemetery is not known.

1837 – A gravestone dating back to this year is located in the cemetery.

Investigation

The cemetery is commonly known as "13 Steps Cemetery" due to the thirteen steps that lead up to the gates of the graveyard.

Others in the area refer to the cemetery as the Lewis Bottoms Cemetery, as many of the graves are from the Lewis family.

In 1997, investigators researching the graveyard reported a ghostly phantom dog running past them. They also reportedly captured a photo of a disappearing house that is sometimes reported by visitors.

Visitors to the cemetery report seeing a green ball of light hovering over the Lewis family gravesites.

Investigators have captured strange voices and noises while walking through the cemetery.

We spoke with several residents of this small town who had all heard of the haunting activity that takes place up at the cemetery.

Many people who have ventured to the graveyard have been touched or pushed by some unseen force.

To dissuade people from visiting the cemetery, workers at the nearby gas station in Palo often purposely give inaccurate directions to those seeking the graveyard.

Eerie unknown human shapes have been reported in the cemetery. We spoke with a man who went out to the cemetery to see for himself if it was haunted. When he got there, he heard the sounds of a little child. This was enough proof for the young man, as he quickly took off out of the cemetery.

Another witness told us that he was visiting the cemetery when he was chased out away by a cult that was performing a ritual in the cemetery.

In 2003, a young man had heard a lot of stories concerning the haunting activity and decided that he had to check out the cemetery for himself. The man talked two friends into accompanying him on his adventure. After a few hours of nothing happening, the group decided to take off. As they got back to their car they noticed a Department of Natural Resources employee pull up to ask them some questions. The DNR man put his truck into park and walked over to the group's car and asked why they were at the cemetery and whether or not they had been drinking. The group stated that they were only there to see the ghost. The DNR employee seemed

like he had heard that explanation too many times and was thinking of giving them a ticket when, from out of nowhere, his truck shifted from park to drive and started to lunge forward. The DNR employee ran after his truck, caught it, and put it back into park. He let the group go with a warning. The odd part of the story is that the truck had an automatic transmission, making it unlikely to have shifted to drive on its own.

The Dare. Park your car near the entrance and enter the cemetery. When you return to your car you will find a raccoon or other animals covering your car.

Hillbilly Homicide

Location: Strawberry Point, Clayton County, Iowa

Directions: From Strawberry Point, go east on E. Mission Rd. Turn left on Eagle Ave. and Mossy Glen is 4 miles north.

Ghost Lore

Many people claim that Mossy Glen has more ghosts per square mile than any other location in Iowa. It is believed that at least five ghosts walk the mossy trails of the glen.

- A man committed suicide by plunging into a muddy sinkhole. His mud-caked apparition walks the area near the bogs.

- A peddler was murdered, decapitated, and robbed by local residents in the 1850s. He haunts the cave where they dumped his body. People have seen him walking through the glen carrying his severed head tucked under his arm.

71

- An attorney's wife died mysteriously. Local people suspected murder. Many believed the young lawyer was being haunted and tormented by her ghost. One day he drove out to Mossy Glen. He disappeared into the darkness, along with his horse and buggy. It is said the vengeful wife still walks the trails.

- Lucinda, a forlorn lover, left behind a single rose on the path near the cliff where she leaped to her death. The dare: If you speak her name three times, she will appear. If she drops a rose at your feet, you are fated to died the very next day.

Pearl Shine

- Pearl Shine was a hillbilly who was convicted of murdering her husband. Apparently, the judges of the Underworld have sentenced her to eternally wander through Mossy Glen.

History

Pearl Hines, a young "hillbilly girl," spent most of her early life in orphanages in Des Moines and Davenport. As an adult, she lived with relatives west of Littleport and north of Strawberry Point in the hilly wilderness, far off the main roads, known as Mossy Glen. She was a red-haired vixen described as plump, big-framed, buxom, or hearty. Some people referred to her as an "Amazon." She was married and divorced twice before the age of 30.

In the spring of 1836, a murder plot unfolded. Pearl had an uncle, James "Jim" Hines, 26, who lived nearby. Jim was the third husband of his common-law wife Minnie Hines, 51. Minnie was described as "wrinkled and shrunken," with "stringy hair falling about her face," and she usually wore a tattered "Mother Hubbard" style dress. Minnie was the mother of 25 children, 18 of whom were still living. She used to tell people, "Don't ask me who each of their fathers are, because I don't even know." Minnie and Jim lived in a log cabin without running water or electricity. All 18 children slept on straw on the upstairs floor.

For three months Pearl worked as a housekeeper for a 56-year-old bachelor Daniel M. Shine, known to locals as "Old Dan." Shine owned an 80-acre farm where he lived with his 70-year-old bachelor brother Timothy.

Jim and Minnie hatched a plot to have Pearl marry Old Dan. They conspired to murder him so Pearl could inherit Dan's farm and money, and be able to help them out financially.

1936 – Thursday, April 30. Pearl had just turned 33 when she married Old Dan Shine.

The Hines family needed a patsy for the murder, so Pearl contacted 18-year-old Maynard Lenox, a gawky, bushy-haired youth she knew from East Dubuque, Illinois. With her wiles she enticed him to come to Iowa. He immediately hopped a freight train which brought him part way, then he eagerly hiked the rest of the way. The two of them made love. She told Maynard she wasn't happy with her elderly husband, but promised if he were "out of the way," she and Maynard could get hitched. He agreed to participate in the murder plot.

Tuesday, May 5. Just five days after Pearl's marriage to Dan, the plan unfolded. Dan's brother Tim was going to be gone for a couple of days visiting some neighbors. Pearl persuaded Dan to sign a deed transferring his 80-acre farm to him, and she filed it that morning.

Maynard Lenox

Jim and Minnie Hines enlisted the help of Minnie's son-in-law, Albert "Deke" Cornwell, a junk dealer from Manchester. Together with Maynard, they went to Dan's house in the afternoon. Jim and Deke picked a fight with Old Dan. They brutally beat him, then Jim knocked him unconscious by cracking him over the head with a beer bottle. Initially they were going to bury him in a fresh grave that they had dug, but then they came up with new plan. Jim and Maynard carried Dan to the upstairs closet. It was prearranged that Maynard would be the one to do the actual killing. So, with a shotgun, the boy shot Dan in the head. Jim and Deke instructed Maynard and Minnie to stand outside the house as lookouts while they arranged the body to make it appear as if Dan had committed suicide.

They carefully wiped the fingerprints off the gun, placed it beside Dan's body. Then, as if constructing a crude Rube Goldberg device, they tied one end of a string to the trigger, wrapped it around the doorknob, and tied the other end to Dan's finger.

Wednesday, May 6. That evening, Dan's brother Tim returned home to find Dan's bloody body slumped over in the closet. The top of his head had been blown off. He contacted the authorities, who initially assumed it was a suicide, but quickly became suspicious when they found blood stains and shot marks outside the closet door. Sheriff L.J. Palas also thought it was strange that there was no evidence that the gun had recoiled and the bullets in the wall didn't line up with the angle of the gun.

Thursday, May 7. Pearl and Maynard were missing, so the police tracked them down and took them into custody. When they questioned the suspects, Pearl and Maynard both confessed that it was murder, but blamed each other. Because the case was complicated, the police initially arrested 10 members of the Hines family. Later, five were released, but Pearl, Maynard, Jim, Minnie, and Deke ended up being charged with murder.

While locked up, the only concern naïve Maynard had was that he would not get back to his home in East Dubuque in time to see the next installment of the movie serial he was interested in. The "lover boy," as the papers referred to him, sat in his cell playing his five harmonicas and showing no remorse for the murder.

July 6, 1936. Pearl Hines Shine was convicted of first-degree murder and sentenced to life in prison at the Rockwell City Women's Reformatory. Maynard Lenox was convicted of second-degree murder and given a 40-year sentence which was extended to a life sentence for perjury on the witness stand. He was imprisoned at Fort Madison State Penitentiary.

Pearl Shine

Albert "Deke" Cornwell was convicted of murder and given a life sentence. He was imprisoned at Fort Madison State Penitentiary. He died in March of 1977 at the age of 80.

James Hines was given a 99-year term in the insane ward at the Anamosa Men's Reformatory.

March 4, 1937. Minnie Hines, the mother of 18 children, had pleaded innocent, but, after 22 hours and 15 minutes of deliberation, the jury convicted her of second-degree murder. When she was sentenced to 10 years to life, she displayed the same stoicism she had shown throughout her entire trial.

1946 – Minnie Hines, 61, completed a 10-year sentence at Rockwell City and was released.

1952 – September 10. Pearl Shine, 49, was released. She was well liked by her cellmates, and they gave her a going away party. She was hired as a domestic in a northern Iowa home. She resided in What Cheer and later Grace Hill, Iowa.

1952 – September 11. Maynard Lenox, 34, was released, and found employment in central Iowa.

1968 – May. Minnie Hines died at the age of 83.

1971 – February 17. Pearl Hines Shine died at the age of 67. She was living in Washington, Iowa, but was a winter visitor to McAllen, Texas for the last nine years of her life. She died the the McAllen General Hospital. Her body was sent back to Washington for services and burial.

1988 – July 1. Maynard Lenox resided in Racine, Wisconsin when he died at the age of 71.

Investigation

Many of the younger people considered the story of the Hillbilly Homicide to be a legend, but some of the older residents we spoke with remembered when the killing happened. We interviewed several people who knew the Hines family.

People insist they have seen the ghost of the red-haired Pearl Shine wandering the wilderness of Mossy Glen.

We have been unable to verify the stories of the lawyer, Lucinda, or the suicide in the bog. Some of the locals do believe the story of the murdered salesman is true, although they insist he was never decapitated. That detail may have originated with a discovery in 1922. Myron Stone, who lived in Mossy Glen near the Fox Cave five miles north of Edgewood, did find a headless, petrified human body in the cave. It was examined by some scientists who were of the opinion that the body was imbedded in the sand and water more than 45,000 years ago. Because the head was presumably not submerged with the rest of the body, exposure to the air caused it to decay, while the rest of the body was in a near perfect state of preservation.

The Unknown Soldier

Location: Vinton, Benton County, Iowa
Address: Evergreen Cemetery, 1002 East Tenth Street,
Vinton, IA 52349-2368
Phone: (319) 472-4816

Directions: Take 9th St. east. The cemetery will be on the
corner of 9th St. and 10th Ave.

Ghost Lore

This unassuming 50-acre cemetery that sits nestled in the woods of
Vinton contains a statue that is surrounded by a long and sordid his-
tory of paranormal activity. At times the stories about Evergreen
Cemetery sound like they are straight out of a scary movie.
However, rest assured that the residents of Vinton are certain these
stories are more fact than fiction.

- Late at night a statue will come to life and explore the graveyard.

- You may catch a glimpse of the headless man roaming the cemetery.

History

1853 – The cemetery was dedicated.

1912 – The statue for unknown soldiers was dedicated.

Investigation

The statue reads "To our boys of 1861-1865." The statue itself is not uncommon, as there are many others standing in graveyards around the United States. The statue is also available in marble, tin, granite, and steel. The Evergreen Cemetery statue was donated by the Women of Relief Core. Over 1,000 people attended the dedication ceremony.

The 50-acre cemetery is owned by the lot owners and is run by a seven-member, self-appointed board of directors.

The stories of the cemetery being haunted have been around for over 50 years. We spoke with a man who remembered hearing stories from his childhood of the statue coming to life and chasing people around the cemetery.

We spoke with a cemetery employee that has worked at the cemetery for over 20 years. In his time at the cemetery he has witnessed many paranormal events firsthand. On one occasion he was work-

ing during the evening when he spotted a headless man walking through the cemetery. The "man" was dressed in blue jeans and a checkered shirt. When the employee tried to get a closer look at the man, the headless figure simply disappeared into thin air. On another occasion, the employee saw what he described as "a man with lighting bursting out of his body."

The cemetery employee is not alone in his sighting, as many visitors to the cemetery report seeing a similar phenomenon. While walking through the cemetery, witnesses have often seen unexplained lightning.

Many curious young people come to the cemetery hoping to spot the headless man walking the grounds, and all too often they get their wish.

Others who visit the cemetery late at night spot strange unknown colored lights floating around the cemetery.

During the day the statue is in possession of both of its eyes. But at night when witnesses look at the statue, they say that it is missing its right eye.

Local lore tells of visitors entering the cemetery late at night only to see the statue of the soldier actually come to life and begin walking around.

The Dare. If you approach the statue and stare at it, the statue will continue to look at you even as you move away out of its line of sight.

Matsell Bridge and Mansion

Location: Viola, Linn County, Iowa

Directions: From County Home Road, turn onto Stone City Road. Follow it until it becomes Matsell Park Road. (There will be signs for Matsell Bridge Natural Area.)

Ghost Lore

Bridges are often rumored to be haunted. Some people believe that bridges represent a metaphysical crossing between the living world and the spirit world. In addition, many cultures believe that spirits cannot cross running water, thus trapping the spirit on one side of the river. But don't worry about getting stuck on Matsell Bridge, because when you approach the bridge over the Wapsipinicon River, you will have a helping hand or two to push you across.

- Your vehicle will be pushed across the bridge by unseen hands.

- Many people believe the bridge is called Matt's Bridge.

History

1853 – George Matsell constructed a 25-room mansion.

1877 – George Matsell passed away.

1925 – The bridge was constructed by Illinois Steel Bridge Co., the WPA, and the Iowa State Highway Commission.

1929 – Gus Matsell, the last Matsell child, passed away. The home was sold to Charles Robbins of Cedar Rapids. After the death of Charles Robbins, his son Lewis sold the property to Fred Witousek, a Cedar Rapids businessman.

1967 – Fred Witousek's widow sold the land to Linn County for $100 per acre.

1967 – The home was run by the County Park Service.

1967 – The Matsell home burned to the ground.

1998 – The Matsell Bridge was added to the National Register of Historic Places.

Investigation

The Matsell Natural Area was named after George Matsell, who in 1853 acquired 3,000 acres through a grant from the government.

The Matsell Natural Area has a long history of people believing it is haunted. Years ago, residents spoke of the haunted Matsell Mansion. Since the mansion no longer exists, the main haunting now seems to revolve around the bridge.

Curious visitors to the bridge report that if you drive to the bridge and shut your vehicle off, an unknown force will push you across the bridge. Those who have been pushed across the bridge often get out of their vehicle to find the handprints on the back of the car.

Beware, local teens believe that if the ghosts of the bridge get angry, they will try to break your windows or even try to push you off of the bridge.

Lori Erickson did extensive research on the Matsell Mansion for her book, *Ghosts of Linn County*. Erickson interviewed a gentleman who ventured out to the mansion while it was still standing. The man and several friends snuck their way into the home through a window. The group had a good look at the inside of the dilapidated building due to the bright moonlight that shined in through the windows. The young men all felt a cold draft originating from one of the rooms. Building up their courage, they peeked in to find the room empty except for a lone rocking chair. The group was amazed to see that the chair was moving back and forth on its own as though someone or something had been rocking in it. As the guys were about to speed off out of the house, the window in the

room came slamming down. Needless to say, the boys left the house quicker than they entered.

Local lore tells many stories about the origin and history of the home. Matsell served as the first police chief of New York City and it is said that Matsell decided to build the house in Viola so he could escape his many enemies back in New York. In New York, Matsell was accused of taking kickbacks and for having his hand in several illegal practices. No accusations were ever proved, although many wondered how he was able to afford a 3,000-acre vacation home on a policeman's salary. According to local history, the Matsell basement was filled with expensive wines and Matsell's parties were legendary throughout the region.

Matsell is said to have hid over half a million dollars in his house. An even more bizarre story states that Mattsell secretly keep one of his daughters locked up in a basement cage. The ghost of the daughter was said to haunt the home while it was still standing.

Those in the area talked about a series of interconnected tunnels that ran under the house. Some speculate that the tunnels were used to smuggle slaves on the Underground Railroad.

Haunted Hardee's

Location: West Union, Fayette County, Iowa
Address: 117 Highway 150 North, West Union, IA 52175-1050
Phone: (563) 422-5411

Ghost Lore

When it comes to Ouija boards, there are a variety of opinions. Debunkers like James Randi and Penn & Teller have ridiculed them; psychics like Edgar Cayce and Suzy Smith have denounced them; and occultists like Aleister Crowley have advocated them.

The word "Ouija" (pronounced "wee-jee") is derived from the French *oui* (for "yes") and the German/Dutch *ja* (also for "yes"). The Ouija board—also known as a talking board, spirit board, or witch board—first became popular during the Spiritualism movement in the mid-19th century.

Letters of the alphabet, numbers, and the words "yes" and "no" are printed on the board. The participants place their fingers on a device known as a planchette which then moves about the board and spells out messages from the spirits.

Does the Ouija board really work? Some young people wanted to find out. They worked at a Hardee's restaurant built on ground that was formerly part of a nearby cemetery. This particular fast food joint had a notorious reputation for haunting activity.

Ouija Board, Ouija Board
By Morrissey (1989)

Ouija board
Ouija board
Ouija board
Would you help me?
Because I still do feel
So horribly lonely

Would you, Ouija board
Would you, Ouija board
Would you help me?
And I just can't find
My place in this world

- Cold spots. Even on warm days or when the restaurant was warm.

- Items mysteriously misplaced, then later reappearing in unexpected places.

- Employees hearing their names whispered or called out, but nobody is there.

History

1988 – The West Union Hardee's was built.

Investigation

Strange things would happen at the Hardee's almost every day. Kari, the manager, knew something was amiss. Employees would hear voices speaking their name, but it wasn't a coworker. Unusual things would happen in the stockroom. Stacks of cups would fall off the shelf. Things would go sliding across the floor. Items would be missing, then later reappear. The workers sensed there was an unseen presence in the restaurant and were becoming concerned.

One night, after work, Kari and some of the other employees decided to hold a séance. They waited until midnight—the witching hour—then met behind the restaurant equipped with their witch board. They asked the board if there was an entity residing in their restaurant, and the response was an immediate "yes." When they inquired as to his name, the planchette spelled out the name "Steve," and indicated that his last name began with a "G."

Through the Ouija board the spirit communicated that he was buried in the nearby cemetery, and he acknowledged being an evil spirit. He was a petty thief who was either fishing or canoeing on the Turkey River when he accidentally drowned back in the 1940s.

The entity kept trying to persuade them to climb onto the roof of the restaurant. Unsure of what his motive was and knowing he was evil, they refused.

When they challenged him to manifest himself, a large, grey gypsy moth suddenly appeared. They estimated the wing span to be 3 1/2 to 4 inches. The message from the talking board acknowledged that this was the spirit. One of the girls in the group began taunting the moth and swearing at it. She was horrified when it responded by flying at her and landing on her head. She brushed it aside and one of her coworkers of imposing stature, a 6' 3" tall boy, stomped on it. The group was stunned when the moth flew off, apparently unharmed. At this point, they decided to pack up the Ouija board and call it quits for the night. Never again did they dabble with the board.

Virgin Mary Cemetery

Location: West Union, Fayette County, Iowa
Official Name: Mount Pleasant Cemetery

Directions: From West Union, go east on Harding Rd. (Hwy 18), turn right on 240th St. (gravel road), turn right on I Ave. The cemetery will be on the immediate left.

Ghost Lore

It is difficult to find this cemetery, which sits in a remote part of the open prairie. A few headstones and a couple of trees are silhouetted against the gray sky. The markers are old and worn. Some are broken beyond repair. Many of the names and dates are no longer legible. The anguish of a difficult life on the brutal prairie seems to cry out from the graves. To the back of the graveyard stands a lone statue of the Virgin Mary. Weathered, stained, and showing signs of vandalism, it seems to be keeping a vigilant watch over the dead.

She has outstretched hands, as if blessing those who rest in the ground. Beneath her foot is the head of a serpent with a forbidden fruit in his mouth. Rumors are whispered that the statue is haunted and the cemetery is cursed.

- The eyes of the statue will look at you and follow you.

- The statue will sometimes move.

- People who visit the cemetery are sometimes cursed and experience car problems afterwards.

History

1846 – Under the terms of a treaty, the Winnebago were forced to surrender their land in the Fayette County area.

1848 – The US army moved the Winnebago to Minnesota. In the spring, Lorenzo Dutton (1826-1915) was one of the first white people to settle in this area. Initially the settlement was known as

Knob Prairie. That fall he explored the territory and discovered a cave, in which he killed eighteen rattlesnakes. To this day the cave is still known as "Dutton's Cave."

1849 – The town of West Union was developed and named by William Wells.

1837 – Fayette County (named after the French general Marquies de Lafayette) was established.

1851 – West Union became the county seat for Fayette County.

1869 – The Mount Pleasant Cemetery was probably started around this time. Lorenzo Dutton and many of the early pioneers are buried there.

Investigation

A few years ago vandals desecrated the cemetery. The youths defaced some of the gravestones, then removed the statue of the Virgin Mary from its pedestal and drove off with it, later abandoning it in a roadside ditch.

By some accounts, authorities later recovered the statue and returned it to the cemetery. Others say shortly after the vandals ditched the statue, they returned to the cemetery to continue their assault on the headstones and were astounded to find the statue was miraculously back on its pedestal. They ran screaming to their car and hightailed it out of there, never to return.

Many people feel they have been cursed by the graveyard. More specifically, they believe their automobiles have been cursed. One night, a group of five young people visited the cemetery on a dare, and shortly thereafter all of them had car problems. The first one ran out of gas and was forced to walk. The second one had a spark explode from their engine. The third one was in an accident and

her car was smashed by a truck. The fourth one had a car that burst into flames because of faulty wiring. And the fifth one wrecked their car when they hit a deer.

Recently, two foolhardy young people visited the cemetery. They were clowning around with the statue and taking pictures of themselves standing on it. Shortly thereafter, both of them totalled their cars in separate car accidents . . . on the very same day.

People have reported the eyes of the statue moving and following them. Some have seen the arms or the head change position. Others have seen movement in the eyes or the head of the serpent. One person described the experience of staring into the face of the statue and seeing it transform into a skeletal face.

The Dare. If you visit the cemetery, your vehicle will be cursed, and you will have car trouble

NORTHWEST IOWA

Abbie Gardner Cabin

Location: Arnolds Park, Dickinson County, Iowa
Mailing Address: P.O. Box 74, Arnolds Park, IA 51331-0074
Phone: (712) 332-7248
Email: gardner@iowaone.net
Admission: Free. Donations are appreciated.
Hours: Noon to 4 p.m. Mon.-Fri., 9 a.m. to 4 p.m. weekends.
Open Memorial Day through September.

Directions: From Hwy. 71 in Arnolds Park turn towards
Arnolds Park Amusement Park. The site is one block west of
the park.

Ghost Lore

Arnolds Park is a widely known weekend getaway providing
tourists with fishing, hiking, golfing, swimming, and of course, the
hugely popular Arnolds Park Amusement Park. With nearly as
many resorts as residents, the last thing you expect to see in

Arnolds Park is the wonderfully preserved historic site of the Spirit Lake Massacre.

- The cabin was Iowa's first tourist attraction.
- The site is haunted by the ghost of a woman who was kidnapped by Native Americans.
- Several of the spirits of the site will follow people home.
- The tragedy of 1857 has left many trapped spirits in the area.

History

1856 to 1857 – The Gardner family moved to Iowa from New York.

1857 – Thirteen-year-old Abbie Gardner was abducted by Native American leader Inkpaduta during the Spirit Lake Massacre.

1857 – Abbie was released after being held for three months.

1857 – Abbie married Cassville Sharp.

1881 – Inkpaduta died in Canada.

1880s – Abbie and Cassville separated.

1891 – Abbie purchased her father's cabin in Arnolds Park.

1895 – The Massacre Monument was dedicated by the 25th General Assembly of Iowa.

1921 – Abbie passed away in Colfax, Iowa.

1921 – The cabin was owned by Albert and Mary Sharp.

1941 – The Iowa Conservation Commission purchased the cabin.

1973 – The cabin was placed in the National Register of Historic Places.

1974 – The State Historical Society of Iowa took over the cabin and started the process of returning it to its 1856 condition.

Investigation

In the summer of 1856, Rowland (Rolland) Gardner and his family made the arduous trek from New York to Iowa on ox-drawn wagons bursting with all their worldly possessions. Once settled in the area, Gardner built a small log cabin on the shores of Lake Okoboji.

The Gardners knew that many Indians still resided in the area but considered them friendly, a mistake that would soon become deadly. In 1857 a band of Sioux Indians migrated to the area led by Chief Inkpaduta. It is safe to say that Inkpaduta was not a fan of the white man.

One evening while eating dinner the Gardners heard the distinct sounds of a Native American war dance. The Gardners made the fateful error of ignoring these warning signs because they had never had any trouble from the Indians. However, the very next morning while they were enjoying a quiet breakfast they received an uninvited guest.

The "guest" was a tall Indian who walked right into the cabin. Startled by their visitors, Mrs. Gardner offered the man a plate of food which he accepted. Moments later 14 more Indians gathered at the cabin looking for food. Mrs. Gardner gave them what little food she could.

The Indians finally left the cabin, but stuck around the area. The Gardners were obviously worried and soon sent two young men from the village off to warn the other settlers. While waiting for the messengers return the Gardners became increasingly more worried not knowing the young men had been shot by the Indians.

Just as the evening sun set, the Indian came back and demanded all of the Gardner's supplies. When Mr. Gardner turned to get their request he was shot in the back and killed. The Indians then killed all of his family sparing only Abbie, the youngest of the Gardner children, and took her prisoner.

For the next few weeks Abbie was forced to watch as the Indians killed several other villagers and took more prisoners. A visitor to the area also witnessed the killings and ran off to warn the other settlers. This time the messenger made it to safety and was able to alert soldiers at Fort Dodge.

There were not enough men at the fort to fight the Indians so they decided to send the men out to bury all settlers who were killed by the Indians. It was a hard winter and several of the men froze to death while on their mission.

Three months later the Indians decided to sell Abbie Gardner back for horses, blankets, tobacco, and some gunpowder. The transaction completed, Abbie was once again free. Soon after her release Abbie, married Cassville Sharp. They had two children.

Years later Abbie left her husband and moved back to her father's cabin in Arnolds Park and opened it as Iowa's first tourist attraction. Abbie would delight and frighten curious visitors with the stories of her capture and experience among the Indians.

The main ghost of the site seems to be that of Abbie Gardner. Many people feel that even after death Abbie continues to roam the area in which she once lived.

Several people have visited the cabin and its surrounding area only to report the feeling that they were surrounded by spirits.

Some visitors get an even more bizarre experience when they return home from the site. The historic site has received several calls from past visitors who believed that a spirit from the site had followed them home. Those who have unknowingly brought home a spirit often report that their furniture has been rearranged by some unseen force.

Psychics often visit the site in hopes of sensing a spirit in the area. Many of them have been overwhelmed with the feelings of death and sadness pouring out from those who met their fate there. Other psychics at the site report sensing the kind and friendly spirit of Abbie.

However, psychics are not the only ones to feel a presence at the site, as we spoke with the director of the site who informed us that many visitors to the area feel that the spirits of those who died in the massacre are still there.

Gypsy Cemetery

Location: Algona, Union Township, Kossuth County, Iowa

Directions: From Hwy. 69 North, turn left on 230th Street (B-30). Then take a right on 100th Ave. Take another right on 260th Street and the cemetery will be on your left.

Ghost Lore

In years past, communities often had negative views of Gypsies. They were seen as poor beggars and thieves. Folks also believed that they were sinister people and that they would make your well go dry, or that a curse from them would dry up all the milk from your cows. Adding to their mysterious nature was the fact than many believed the Gypsies possessed supernatural powers and psychic abilities.

- The cemetery is guarded by a flock of mysterious crows.

- No matter what the weather is when you get there, it will start raining while you are at the cemetery.

- Ghostly figures of past Gypsies roam this rural cemetery.

- If you cross the old Gypsy fence marker you will be cursed.

History

1800s – Gypsies would often travel through the area camping at their favorite spot along the river.

According to research done by a descendant that was published in 1962 in the *Algona Kossuth County Advance*, the cemetery was started as a private family burial ground by Albert Frink.

1891 – Albert died. Per his wishes, he was to be buried on the land. His wife was informed that he could not be buried there so she sold the land to Union Township with the understanding that a cemetery would be created there, so Albert could be laid to rest.

1893 – The purchase of the land for Union Cemetery was completed. It is also believed that Charles Gutzell, who was a member of the nomadic tribe, died and was buried there as well.

1896 – Alonzo Gutzell, a member of the traveling Gypsies, died of tuberculosis. He was buried in the Union Cemetery.

1911 – Oliver Gutzell, brother to Alonzo was brought to the area for burial by his brother.

1912 – A small iron gate was constructed around the burial plots of the Gypsies.

1912 – The leader of the tribe known as the "Old Queen" passed away and she and her grandson Albert Jeffrey were buried. A ceremony was performed by Rev A.H. Wood.

1924 to 1926 – Mr. Frink wrote that he recalled his father going to the cemetery and finding that all the Gypsies' graves were dug up and the bodies removed.

1968 – Iowa Governor Norman Erbe suggested that the town of Algona use the Gypsy Cemetery as a tourist attraction to bring tourists and their money into the area.

Investigation

Gladys Tribon wrote a story using her sister's name, Ruth, for the *Des Moines Register* stating that originally the Gypsies wanted to bury their loved ones in the Catholic Cemetery. However, the Catholic Church denied the request, so the group had no option but to use the Union Cemetery.

An interesting note about the cemetery is that the old rusted iron-gate door surrounding the Gypsy section of the cemetery was not built to open. Many believe that it was constructed to keep the spirits of their loved ones safe from any outside harm.

The death of young Alonzo was much more interesting than first noted. Many claim that the group of nomadic travelers, following their old customs for burying the dead, performed a burial ritual to help the soul of Alonzo travel into the unknown world of death. The group was said to have spent the whole night chanting, dancing, yelling, singing, and moaning over the body of young Alonzo. The group also held the superstitious belief that it is was unlucky for someone to die on the area they camped on. Following this belief, the very next morning, they loaded up their wagons and put Alonzo onto an old mattress and left him on the side of the road. Soon, nearby resident Frank Riebhiff happened upon this unusual scene. He asked them what they were going to do with the body. As far as they were concerned, they told him, they had already performed the ritual to free the spirit from the body and all that was left was the shell. However, Frank did not see it that way and he tried to convince them that they could not just leave the child there. He informed them that the boy must have a proper burial. The group headed by the Old Queen did not budge and it wasn't until Frank threatened to contact law enforcement officials that his body was moved to the cemetery.

The Old Queen was said to be a master beggar, often begging for one item at a time until she had gotten all the items needed for a meal.

Seven trees were once buried in the cemetery, one for each of the bodies interred there. The graves of the fallen Gypsies were still in the cemetery in the early 1920s.

When Mr. Frink noticed that a group of crows were hovering over the cemetery as though they were on watch patrol, he investigated and found that all the Gypsy bodies had been dug up and were missing. He also discovered heavy wagon tracks and many foot-prints, leading him to believe that the group of nomadic travelers had finally come back for their family.

In 1994, Steve Gansen wrote a story on two men looking to find any evidence of ghostly activity within the cemetery. The two men were Dale Hansmeier and Dave Lehman. The two men visited the site and noticed a large group of crows welcoming their approach. The men also stated that upon their entrance into the cemetery, rain began to fall around them.

We spoke with several residents who informed us that they had heard stories of the cemetery being haunted by the ghosts of the Gypsy people.

The librarians we talked with mentioned that they get a lot of curious people coming in to ask them about the haunted cemetery.

Residents who live in the area have reported seeing some type of strange ceremonies or séances being conducted under cover of darkness.

The Dare. If you are brave enough to walk over the old iron Gypsy fence in the middle of the cemetery, you will be forever cursed by the Gypsy people.

Kate Shelley Memorial Bridge

Location: Boone, Boone County, Iowa

Directions: Go north on Marion Street past 11th Street to 198th Road. Turn left on 198th onto the blacktop road. It will lead you to the bridge. (There will be plenty of signs.)

Ghost Lore

We all wonder what we would do when faced with a moment of truth. Would we freeze up? Or would we rise to the occasion and be heroic? Luckily most people never have to face that situation. The same cannot be said for 15-year-old Kate Shelley who, when faced with adversity, made the decision to . . . well you'll see.

- The bridge Kate saved is haunted by her ghost.

- A dim lantern has been spotted floating along the tracks.

109

- Phantom trains have been seen and heard over the bridge.

History

1865 – Kate Shelley was born.

1881 – A major storm blew through Moingona taking out a trestle, forcing a railroad car into the Honey Creek.

1881 – Fifteen-year-old Kate Shelley saved the train track by crawling across a bridge.

1883 – Kate attended Simpson College.

1890 – Kate's family was given $917.05 from the *Chicago Tribune* to build a new home.

1891 – Kate's new home was finished.

1901 – The Kate Shelley High Bridge opened.

1912 – Kate passed away.

1930s – The original bridge Kate saved was demolished.

2002 – The Kate Shelley Bridge underwent major renovations allowing new trains to pass over it.

Investigation

A devastating storm passed through Moingona. The storm blew out a trestle on the bridge. However, the oncoming #11 train car was unaware of damage and rushed over the bridge—falling into the river—drowning two crewmembers and stranding two others. Upon seeing the disaster Kate decided to battle the elements and crawl across the bridge to warn oncoming trains of the bridge failure. After crawling on her hands and knees the length of two football fields Kate finally reached the other side. Not only was Kate able to warn the train, she helped lead the rescue party to help the stranded crew.

Overnight Kate became a national hero. The state of Iowa gave her a gold medal created by Tiffany Jewelers. She was also honored with the naming of her own bridge. The Kate Shelley Bridge is the longest and highest double-track bridge in the world. It stands a staggering 185 feet tall and runs over 2,685 feet.

Many people erroneously believe that the Kate Shelley Bridge is the bridge that she saved in 1881. The bridge Kate saved has long since been demolished. However, you can still get to where the old bridge was by visiting the Kate Shelley Museum.

Several residents at the railroad museum informed us that they heard the place was haunted by the ghosts of several workers who fell to their deaths during construction of the bridge.

Witnesses have reported seeing a small lantern moving along the rails as though some unseen force were carrying it. Many of those who have seen the light believe that it is the ghost of Kate Shelley continuing to roam the bridges of Iowa.

Other witnesses report seeing and hearing what they think are train cars moving along the tracks, yet upon further inspection no trains can be found. These phantom cars have been spotted during both day and night.

American Theatre

Location: Cherokee, Cherokee County, Iowa
Address: 108 East Main Street, Cherokee, IA 51012-1850
Phone: (712) 225-2345
Email: renea@fridleytheatres.com
Website: www.fridleytheatres.com/cherokee.html

Directions: From Hwy. 59 turn east onto Main Street. The theatre is on the left.

Ghost Lore

People go to the movies for a variety of reasons. Some go for a short escape from their lives, while others simply go to be entertained. Still others go to the movies to be scared. However, movie-goers usually expect to be scared by the movie, not the theatre itself. That is not the case at the American Theatre, where visitors believe the movie could never be as scary as the ghosts who still hang around there.

- Mr. Goldie, a former owner of the theatre, still haunts his old business.

- Theatre seats are seen moving on their own.

- The eerie basement was once used as a bomb shelter.

History

1920s – The building was constructed.

1923 – Barry and Sick's company went bankrupt.

1923 – The *Cherokee Chief* reported that Mr. Goldie purchased the theatre for $2,200 at auction.

1925 – Dale and Hazel Goldie opened the American Theatre.

Currently – The American Theatre is still operating.

Investigation

Several men sought to bring a theatre to the community. They began work on the American Theatre on Main Street. However the men ran out of money before it was completed. The theatre was put up for sale at a sheriff's auction. Dale Goldie and his wife purchased the theatre at the auction and ran it for many years.

On our tour we were told that the basement once served as a Civil Defense Fallout Center. Although the Historical Society doubted that it was ever used as a shelter, the theatre staff were said to have found evidence of its use while cleaning the basement.

A former manager was doing a routine screening of a movie that was to open during the weekend. Alone in the dark theatre the manager heard a chair start squeaking as though someone had sat down in it. Startled by the noise, the man peeked over at the empty seat and was amazed to see that it was moving on its own. The man was completely shocked at what he had just witnessed and darted out of the theatre.

The new manager has been here for over five years and has not had a paranormal experience.

An employee was threading film for a showing when he saw someone behind him. When he turned around to see who had entered the room, he was baffled to find that he was alone.

Several of the employees shared with us their fears of going into the basement because of their belief that it is haunted. Many other employees reported getting an eerie feeling when in the basement.

In 2001, several ghost researchers were in the theatre and reportedly captured several orbs on their photographs.

One employee was taking photos in the theatre for a photography class. After the photos were developed, she was surprised to notice several orbs in her pictures.

A private party was taking place in the theatre when several of the guests reported an eerie cold chill running over them even though the theatre was sufficiently heated.

The Day the Music Died

Location: Clear Lake, Cerro Gordo County, Iowa

Directions: From Route 18 in Clear Lake head north on Eight St. (Rt. S28) for approximately five miles. Turn right on onto the dirt road which is 310th St. Turn left onto Gull Avenue. At the intersection of 315th St. and Gull Avenue, you will need to walk along the fence for a half-mile to find the memorial for the crash.

Ghost Lore

Imagine a simple flip of a coin deciding whether you will live or die. That was the case for the tragic crash that is best known as "the day the music died." Fate seemed to be against the men who took off in the plane heading for their next show. Fans of the musicians take solace in the fact that the music continues to live on after the death of their idols. However, others believe that their music isn't the only thing that continues to live on.

- Ghosts of the famous singers still roam the area where they died.

- Mysterious figures have been spotted along the secluded road.

History

1959 – The plane carrying Buddy Holly, Richie Valens, and J.P. Richardson "The Big Bopper" crashed into an Iowa corn field.

1959 – The pilot of the plane, Roger Peterson, was buried in the Buena Vista Memorial Cemetery in his hometown.

1959 – Ritchie Valens' body was moved from the Noble Chapel Funeral Home to San Fernando Mission Cemetery.

1959 – Buddy Holly was buried in Lubbock, Texas.

1980 – Holly's glasses and some other effects were found in an evidence envelope.

1998 – The memorial was constructed in the corn field.

Investigation

According to research by Gary Thelen: Waylon Jennings, Buddy Holly, Ritchie Valens, and the Big Bopper, along with their bands, were on "The Winter Dance Party" tour. The tour was one long cold Midwest road trip. Among the many difficulties was the fact that their bus kept breaking down and oftentimes the heat was not available. Due to the poor travel conditions several band members had caught colds and one even developed frostbite.

The groups had just finished their gig at the Surf Ballroom when a sick Buddy Holly decided that he did not want ride the old tour bus to Moorhead, Minnesota. Holly arranged to charter a plane to Fargo, North Dakota, the closest town they could fly to for their next gig.

The problem was that the plane could only hold two other passengers. Band member Waylon Jennings ended up volunteering to give his seat to the Big Bopper, and Bob Hale flipped a coin to see if Ritchie Valens or Tommy Alsup would get the last spot on the warm plane. Valens won the coin flip that would seal his fate.

Holly then used the pay phone outside the Surf Ballroom to call his brother. While leaving Holly took the opportunity to rib Jennings, who had given up his seat. Holly joked, "You're not going on that plane with me tonight?" Jennings simply said "No." Buddy kept on teasing and said, "Well, I hope your old bus freezes up again." Jennings looked at his friend and jokingly replied, "Well, I hope your old plane crashes." Little did the men know that both their predictions would come true that night.

The three musicians took off on a four-passenger Beechcraft Bonanza. The plane was piloted by Roger Peterson who was an inexperienced 21-year-old pilot. The men left from the Surf Ballroom in Clear Lake heading to the Mason City Airport. A storm warning for the area did not reach the pilot. At approximately 1:00 a.m., the small plane crashed into the cornfield of Albert Juhl, killing everyone on board.

When the plane did not arrive in Fargo, people started to worry. The next day Jerry Dwyer mounted a search party and found the plane's wreckage along a snow-covered field. A doctor showed up, as did the press and curious passersby.

The bodies were removed and buried at their various hometowns. However, this is only the beginning of the story. Once the ground thawed, the farmer found several plane parts, some personal items, along with a few stray body parts.

In 1988, a Buddy Holly fan from Wisconsin constructed a memorial at the site of the crash.

The name of the plane was not American Pie, as is widely believed.

Some say Holly's glasses were actually found by a farmer who was plowing his field 20 years after the crash.

Drivers of the area have reported seeing the ghosts wandering the farm area where the plane crashed in 1959. The witnesses believe that the ghosts are those of Buddy Holly, the Big Bopper, and Ritchie Valens.

Strange noises have also been heard in the area. The unknown noises sound as though a plane were crashing into the farmland.

Humboldt County Historical Museum

Location: Dakota City, Humboldt County, Iowa
Address: 905 First Avenue North, Dakota City, IA 50548-1701
Phone: (515) 332-5280

Directions: From 8th Street turn left onto 1st Avenue.

Ghost Lore

Every town seems to have an old dilapidated home with which everyone is familiar. Complete with broken out windows, boarded up doors, and an overrun yard, the home quickly gets a reputation of being haunted. However, what happens when that old rundown house gets renovated back to its former glory? Do people still believe the home to be haunted? Well, many residents of Dakota City would answer yes.

- The building is haunted by World Champion wrestler Frank Gotch.

- The sign in front of the building will sway in the wind in answer to your questions.

- Mysterious lights have been seen while the museum is empty.

History

1878 – The home was built in the Italian style with bricks gathered from the nearby Des Moines River. The home was constructed by Corydon Brown, Sr. He made his fortune in milling. Brown lived in the home with his wife, Lucelia Stevens Brown. The family moved away from the area. Due to neglect and time the home fell victim to deterioration.

1966 – The Art Kunerts and Mrs. Clarence Kunert donated the home and adjoining land to the Humboldt County Historical Association.

1968 – Many volunteers helped restore the home to its original glory. The home was re-vamped and opened to the public.

1979 – The Mill Farm House was the first building in Humboldt County to be listed on the National Register of Historic Places by the Iowa State Historical Department.

Investigation

The home is frequently referred to as the Mill Farm House, the Corydon Brown House, and the Historical Museum House of Dakota City. It contains an 1883 schoolhouse, a doctor's office, a jail, and a post office.

We spoke with the director who has been at the home for more than eight years. She said that she could not recall a reason why the home is said to be haunted.

The director reported that she was alone in an upstairs bedroom when she witnessed the window shade go flipping up on its own. She said she believed that it must have been moved the day before when the room was cleaned.

The director also stated that she often gets an odd, eerie feeling while alone in the house, but chalks it up to just being alone in an old home. She feels that if there is a spirit in the house that it is a friendly spirit.

Frank Gotch was an undefeated wrestling champion of the early 1900s. Gotch died in 1917 at age 39, and although the museum does contain many mementoes from the wrestling legend, they do not believe that his ghost is haunting the place. Staff members believe that if the ghost of Gotch was haunting a building in Dakota City, he would probably be haunting his old home which is still standing in town.

Many longtime residents of Dakota City remember growing up calling the home "the haunted house" due to its rundown appearance and broken windows.

Several residents reported that years ago, when they would drive by the old home during the evening, they would see lights being turned on and off even though the home was supposed to be empty and abandoned.

The Dare. If you ask a question while standing in front of the museum sign, the sign will reply with movement. This is said to happen on even the stillest of nights. Just for your reference, if the sign moves right, the answer to your question is yes, and if it moves left, the answer is no.

Vacant Lot

Location: Emmetsburg, Palo Alto County, Iowa

Directions: Take 18 east out of town (Main Street), turn right on Huron. The old vacant lot will be on the right behind Nauss Oil.

Ghost Lore

Throughout this book you will see haunted cemeteries, theatres, bridges, statues, and many more locations. But you will only read about one vacant lot in the whole book. This brings up the question of whether a haunting can still linger around after an establishment has long been removed. Well, many people in Emmetsburg believe that the owner of a former business is still checking in his customers.

- A hotel once sat on this land and is the cause for the haunting.

- An elderly man is often seen wailing the vacant lot.

History

Little is known about the hotel that once stood on the land. What is known is that it was called the Gunn Hotel. We do not know when the hotel was constructed.

The hotel was owned by Elmer and Joyce Gunn.

1960s – Many residents remember the hotel being open during this time.

Late 1960s – Many residents remember the hotel as being extremely run down during this time.

1970s – The hotel finally closed down.

Investigation

The vacant lot is located behind Nauss Oil. The former oil company is also closed down, yet the building still remains.

Many people tell the story of a Motor Lodge Motel being on this site. It was not the Motor Lodge Hotel, as it was the Gunn Hotel.

There are several Gunns that live in the area.

We spoke with a long time resident that reported that toward the end of the hotel's life it was a bit run down and did not know why anyone would have stayed there unless they had to.

Although the hotel is no longer standing, witnesses still report seeing an elderly man in a plaid shirt walking around the lot.

The ghostly man that is often spotted appears to be conducting a daily check of the phantom hotel doors. Witnesses report that it appears as though the man believes the hotel is still operating and is concerned for the safety of his guests.

Oak Hill Cemetery

Location: Estherville, Emmet County, Iowa

Directions: From Central Avenue, turn left on WS 1st Street, then turn right on W 2nd Ave. S. The Cemetery will be on the left at the top of the hill.

Ghost Lore

When people think of who may be haunting a cemetery, they often believe that the place is haunted by those buried in their final resting place. It is a rare occurrence that a cemetery is said to be haunted by several people who died on the road outside of the cemetery. Yet, Oak Hill Cemetery is one such place.

- Football players who died outside of the cemetery still haunt the area.

- Two young girls who died on the cemetery road continue to play on the road, even after their deaths.

- If you stop, mysterious ghosts will push your vehicle uphill until you are safe from oncoming cars.

History

1856 – The area of Estherville was first settled.

1881 – Estherville was incorporated as a city.

1889 – The cemetery was established. The city was named after Esther Ridley who was the wife of Estherville's founder Robert Ridley. Both are buried at Oak Hill Cemetery.

Investigation

The main story of the haunting revolves around a carload of football players. It is said that the group of high school football play-

ers were on their way to a big game against a rival school when their car broke down on the hill next to Oak Hill Cemetery. In a hurry to get to the game, they started pushing the car up the hill. While pushing the car, another car raced by from the opposite direction and stuck the players, killing them instantly.

Another version of the haunting circulating throughout the area focuses on two small girls who are said to be haunting the road.

Even with the help and local expertise of the *Estherville Daily News,* we were unable to find any story of football players dying up at Oak Hill Cemetery.

The stories of the graveyard being haunted have lingered for at least 30 years.

We spoke with a psychic woman who reported getting cold chills at the cemetery. She believed that the odd feelings were due to several alleged witches buried there. She refused to go up to the cemetery again.

Those who travel to the cemetery report seeing mysterious eyes floating through the graveyard. We spoke with two women who stated that the color of the eyes frequently changes.

The Dare. Drive your car up to the cemetery and park it on the flat area of the road. When you put your car into neutral, your car will be pushed uphill by the ghostly unseen hands of the football players (or the young girls).

Hawkeye Community Theatre

Location: Fort Dodge, Webster County, Iowa
Address: 521 North Twelfth Street, Fort Dodge, IA 50501-3246
Mailing Address: P.O. Box 32, Fort Dodge, IA 50501-0032
Email: hawkeyetheatre@hotmail.com
Phone: (515) 576-6061

Directions: From 5th Ave. (US-20 BUS) turn right onto 12th St. and you will see the theatre.

Ghost Lore

Theatres are often thought to be haunted and there may be several reasons for that reputation. First, theatres usually have a lot of costumes and props giving way to skeptics who claim witnesses are actually seeing these props and not real ghosts. Others believe that those who participate in theatre often do it for their love of it and when they pass away they want to continue doing what they loved while they were alive. Another theory is that castmembers and theatre audiences generate a lot of energy that attracts spirits to them. Regardless of whether you believe the theories, the people at the Hawkeye Community Theatre believe their theatre is haunted.

- The ghost of a little girl has been spotted in the theatre.
- Mysterious noises have been heard echoing around the theatre.

History

1895 – Christian Science was introduced in Fort Dodge.

1917 – The building was constructed to be used as the First Church of Christ Scientist.

1957 – The Hawkeye Community Theatre was created. The first play was *Heaven Can't Wait.*

1958 – The group performed in the Webster County 4-H building.

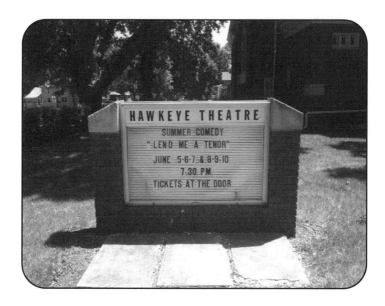

1961 – A play was housed in the North Junior High Auditorium.

1964 – The need for a permanent home for the group was mentioned by the director.

1982 – The group celebrated 25 years of community theatre.

1994 – The theatre moved to the Colonial Inn.

2000 – The theatre moved into its permanent location.

2004 – The theatre is honored by the Historical Society for the preservation and adaptive use of a historic building.

Investigation

An interesting fact of the building is that when it served as a church, not one marriage or funeral took place inside its walls. The former members of the church did not believe that a church was the place for those events.

We spoke with a member of the board of directors who informed us that many people believe that the ghost of the theatre is that of a male.

The stories of the place being haunted seemed to have started in 1999, when the theatre took over the building.

Community members who have attended an event in the theatre have reported a strange feeling of being watched by someone or something.

Many of the longtime volunteers of the theatre have had paranormal experiences.

We spoke with a volunteer who works a lot of nights in the theatre on his own, and although he had never seen a ghost, he stated that there are plenty of spooky nooks and crannies for something to hide.

Many of the volunteers have reported seeing a ghostly figure floating through the back rooms of the theatre.

During October the theatre has set up several haunted houses for the community to visit. What is strange is that most of the children are more afraid of the building than of the volunteers who are dressed up as monsters inside.

The Devil's Chair

Location: Guthrie Center, Guthrie County, Iowa

Directions: Take State Street to the east. The cemetery will be on your left. The chair is located in the middle of the cemetery.

Ghost Lore

What harm could come from visiting a cemetery and taking a rest in the comfortable chair that is just sitting there? Isn't that what a chair is for? Well unless you are in need of some bad luck, you may want to re-think plopping down in the Devil's Chair of Union Cemetery, because many believe the chair is cursed.

Those who have sat in the chair have been cursed with otherwise inexplicable bad luck.

History

1885 – The graveyard was laid out by a county surveyor.

William and Margaret Hammond created the cemetery as a private burial ground.

Guthrie Center purchased the cemetery from the Hammonds. There were already several graves in the cemetery when the city purchased it.

Investigation

No one in town seemed to know the name of the town cemetery. The cemetery's official name is the Union Cemetery.

There is no inscription on the chair. However, the chair is placed between the Miller and Peterson gravestones and may be a memorial to either one.

We spoke with a cemetery employee who grew up in Guthrie Center. He reported that the legend of the chair has been around for at least 30 years.

A young man told us that if you are brave enough to sit in the chair you will experience a case of bad luck. When asked whether or not he had ever sat in the chair, the man replied that even though he didn't believe in such things he wasn't going to tempt fate.

Rainbow Bridge

Location: Lake City, Calhoun County, Iowa

Directions: From 175 W (Main Street) turn left on Rainbow Road. At the "T" turn right on 365th Street. Take the first left on Iberia Avenue. When you cross the bridge the Rainbow Bridge will be on your right.

Ghost Lore

How many reasons do you need to inspire you to make the trip to a bridge? How about the fact that it is an odd looking bridge out in the middle of nowhere? Not interested? Ok, now add the fact that it is the only bridge of it kind in the United States. Still not interested? Ok, finally add the fact that the bridge is believed to haunted and you have yourself a must-visit site.

History

1914 – The bridge was constructed by the Iowa Bridge Company out of Des Moines.

1985 – The bridge ceased being used for vehicles.

1989 – The bridge was listed as an Iowa Historic Site and placed on the National Register of Historic Places.

1995 – The bridge was documented by *Historic American Engineering Record.*

Investigation

The bridge is also known as Coon River Bridge and Rainbow Bend Access.

The triple span Marsh arch concrete bridge is thought to be the only surviving three-span bridge.

Strange noises often accompany visitors while they are at the bridge. These noises have not been identified.

We spoke with many residents in town who were aware of the bridge and the belief that it was haunted.

The Dare. At midnight bring an unopened candy bar and set it in the middle of the bridge. Make sure you leave the bridge for five minutes and when you return you will find the candy bar is gone and the unopened wrapper still there.

Mount Hope Cemetery

Location: Madrid, Boone County, Iowa

Directions: From town take Hwy 17 N (Kennedy Ave). The cemetery will be on your right.

The gravestones are located in the left side of the middle section of the cemetery.

Ghost Lore

Many cemeteries have multiple family members buried in them. Often families enjoy the thought of being placed next to their loved ones. Mt. Hope Cemetery is no different except that several members of one family like to make their presence known to visitors.

- The ghost of a young girl named Sarah will follow you around the cemetery.

- An unknown child's voice can be heard coming from the gravestones.

History

1870 – The land was first used as a cemetery. Little is known about the early history of the graveyard.

1901 – The cemetery was first officially incorporated for the use of burial.

1901 – The cemetery was surveyed by a group of women called the M.B. Club.

1921 – A new addition was added to the cemetery by the M.B. Club.

1921 – The cemetery was reorganized and new articles of incorporation were drawn up.

1921 – The cemetery was switched to a public cemetery for the town of Madrid.

Investigation

The gravestones are actually those of the Williams family. There are numerous graves of the Williams family including:

> **Ben Williams**
> Died Feb. 22, 1884.
>
> **Hanna Williams**
> Died 1871 at the age of 13.
>
> **Charles A. Williams** (Son of F.E. Williams)
> Died 1870 at 11 years old.
>
> **Sarah C. Williams**
> Died – At age 8. (Year not legible.)
>
> **Sarah J. Williams**
> Date unknown.
>
> **Ailey Ann Williams** (Wife of Ben Williams)
> Died 1850 at age 31 years.

Another grave markers of an infant who died in 1858 is too worn to make out exact details.

It is believed that the ghost of Sarah haunts the cemetery. However you can see that there are two girls named Sarah, both spelled with an "h."

Visitors who travel to the cemetery often report that while they are walking through the graves some unseen force will tug at their clothes.

Several people have gone to the cemetery after hearing that it is haunted only to hear a child's voice. The voice appears to follow people as they move around the graveyard.

East Lawn Cemetery

Location: Sheldon, O'Brien County, Iowa

Directions: Turn left on E 9th Street and the cemetery will be on your left.

Ghost Lore

Oftentimes finding a loved one's gravestone is quite the chore in a large cemetery. All the gravestones start to blend together in a sea of granite and marble. Now imagine that you are searching for the gravestone of a person who was buried before the cemetery was even created. That is the challenge you will have at the East Lawn Cemetery. For an even greater challenge, visit the cemetery at midnight and you may find a ghostly visitor moving about.

- A white shadowy figure roams the cemetery late at night.

- An odd grave in the cemetery is inexplicably older than the cemetery itself.

History

1881 – Mayor Wykoff purchased a 10-acre site for $400.

1881 – The cemetery was started.

1893 – The arches of the cemetery were constructed by the concerned ladies of Sheldon. The cemetery organization raised $400 under the leadership of Mesdames Sleeper.

Investigation

The cemetery is also widely known as 9th Street Cemetery.

Although the cemetery did not originate until 1881, there is a gravestone bearing the name "Lottie" that dates back to 1873. No

one seems to know how a grave could have been placed in the cemetery before it was an official cemetery. One theory is that the young woman was originally buried somewhere else and her remains were reburied once the East Lawn Cemetery was created.

The old Catholic Cemetery is located across the street.

Local lore tells of people venturing into the cemetery at midnight. While they are in the cemetery, they report seeing a strange, floating shadowy figure. Upon investigation, no cause for the figure is ever found.

Graceland Cemetery

Location: Sioux City, Woodbury County, Iowa

Directions: From Gordon Drive (20) take a right on S. Lake Port.

Ghost Lore

If you like roaming around cemeteries, then this one is certainly for you. With over 25,000 graves, this cemetery is simply huge. Filled with odd stones, unique history, and a former Iowa governor buried there, it is no wonder the cemetery receives so many visitors. Many visitors travel to the cemetery because they believe it is haunted, and as you will see, they have good reason.

• Cameras will mysteriously stop functioning while inside the graveyard.

- Strange orbs of light have appeared on the film of those who are able to get their cameras to work.

- Visitors experience disorientation while walking in the cemetery.

History

1909 – The Graceland Cemetery was established by A.M. Jackson.

1912 – The Graceland Chapel was built for $32,800.

1917 – A white marble mausoleum was constructed at a price of over $100,000.

1943 – Mr. Jackson passed away. The cemetery began to decline.

1951 – The cemetery was placed into receivership.

1951 – A lawsuit was brought against the Graceland Cemetery Association alleging misappropriations of funds. To resolve the suit, Mr. Snyder was appointed as a receiver.

1953 – The Graceland Cemetery Association was reorganized to look into transferring the cemetery to the city.

1953 – The city accepted ownership of Graceland Cemetery.

Investigation

The cemetery was designed by landscape architect Charles M. Finley for use as a private cemetery. It was privately owned until the founder, Mr. Jackson, passed away. Judge Forsling approved the deed and authorized the clerk of the district court to deliver the cemetery deed to the city.

During the early 1900s Graceland Cemetery was so highly regarded that people came from hundreds of miles away to purchase a plot.

Thousands of people came from neighboring states to witness the dedication of the mausoleum in the cemetery. The main address during the dedication was delivered by Governor W.L. Harding.

We spoke with an employee of the cemetery who informed us that numerous college kids call the cemetery looking for information about it being haunted.

Paranormal investigators have claimed to have captured strange orbs on their film while investigating the cemetery.

Others are not so lucky, some complaining that while inside the cemetery, for some unknown reason, their cameras will not function.

KD Station

Location: Sioux City, Woodbury County, Iowa

Directions: From Cunningham Drive turn on Leech Road and the KD Station will be on the right.

Ghost Lore

The idea of touring a dilapidated old slaughterhouse brings shivers to many people. Walking among the leftover blood, bones, and animal body parts may not seem too appealing, but don't worry . . . the days of cattle meeting their fate in the building are long gone. The old KD slaughterhouse now enjoys an equally bloody reputation as a haunted building.

- A tragic accident at the slaughterhouse killed several workers who continue to haunt the building.

- So many odd things happen in the building that they have even advertised the ghost on their flyer.

- Elevators have been seen operating on their own.

History

1920 – The Swift and Company packinghouse was constructed.

1949 – A tragic gas explosion killed 21 workers.

1974 – Swift and Company moved to a new location in the city and the building closed down.

1975 – Kermit Lohry looked to turn the building into shopping boutiques and a recreation area.

1976 – The first shops of the KD Station were opened.

1977 – Forty-one more shops opened.

Currently – The dilapidated old cattle stockyard is closed and is under consideration for demolition. City officials are looking into securing funds from the Environmental Protection Agency to remove the asbestos.

Investigation

The KD Stockyards are located in the district along the Floyd River. It was one of the largest commercial livestock businesses in the country. Swift & Company and Armour & Company were two very large livestock companies that operated in the stockyards.

During the heyday of the stockyard, many supplemental businesses including a western wear store, lumberyard, restaurant, and saloon provided customers with all their needs.

An article by Jesse Claeys quotes a former tenant of the building who stated that the owner always thought that the place was haunted by Paul Pulaski.

At one point the ghostly haunting was advertised in one of the building's brochures. The brochure read, "Paul Pulaski, our in-house ghost welcomes you."

In 1949 Swift & Company experienced a tragic accident when 21 employees were killed by an explosion. The incident took place in the packing house and although the cause was never confirmed, it was believed to have been the result of a leaking gas pipe.

Many of the women who worked in the building believed that the building was haunted. The women frequently got an eerie feeling that they were never alone in the building.

Visitors reported hearing the elevators moving up and down, yet when they went to investigate they found that the elevator was not moving at all.

We spoke with several residents who believed that those who had ghostly experiences in the building were just hearing and seeing the cattle of the stockyard.

Visitors who went to the station when it was a recreation area reported seeing items from the explosion still being displayed on the walls.

Unusual noises are reported throughout the building. The noises often sound like old machines running, although no source for the eerie noises has been found.

Sioux City Airport

Location: Sioux City, Woodbury County, Iowa
Address: 2403 Ogden Avenue, Sioux City, IA 51111
Phone: (712) 279-6165
Fax: (712) 277-8287
Website: www.flysiouxgateway.com

Directions: Take I29 South and follow the signs.

Ghost Lore

The fear of flying is a common condition for most travelers. We all hope that the plane we are traveling in does not crash. Passengers aboard Flight 232 experienced that fear first hand when their plane went down. Fortunately, not everyone on board Flight 232 died. Over 150 passengers survived the crash. Others were not so lucky and did not. Many believe their spirits continue to roam the airport waiting for their next flight.

159

Mysterious screams and moans still linger throughout the airport.

History

1989 – United Flight 232 took off from Denver to Chicago.

1989 – Flight 232 crashed on the Sioux City Gateway Airport.

1994 – A statue depicting Dennis Nielsen was constructed near the Anderson Dance Pavilion.

2006 – Surviving passenger Michael Matz trained the Kentucky Derby winner.

Investigation

United Flight 232 took off on July 19, 1989 from Stapleton International Airport in Colorado bound to Chicago International Airport with 285 passengers when it underwent an engine failure of its number two engine. Unable to maneuver, the pilot lost control and the plane crashed into the Sioux City Airport killing 110 passengers and 11 crewmembers.

One hundred seventy-five passengers and 10 crew members survived the tragic crash. Extremely well-trained rescue crews were credited with so many people surviving the crash.

The cause of the crash was originally blamed on poor maintenance by the airline. The follow-up investigation concluded that the crash was caused by a faulty part.

The plane crash was the subject of a TV movie. In 1992 the movie *Crash Landing: The Rescue of Flight 232* aired. The crash was also featured on the National Geographic Channel's *Seconds From Disaster* show.

Captain Haynes believed there were three reasons why so many people survived the crash. First was that the crash occurred during the daylight hours. Second was that the crash took place during a shift change at the regional trauma center and the burn center providing twice the number of personnel on hand to help the survivors. Lastly, the Iowa National Guard was on duty at the airport.

Visitors to the airport reported hearing strange sounds of people screaming along with mysterious moans. These noises are believed to be from the spirits of the victims of Flight 232.

Travelers report seeing unknown figures moving around the airport even though no source has been found.

Vegors Cemetery

Location: Stratford, Hamilton County, Iowa

Directions: Take Highway 175 to the west. Turn right on Bellville. Turn right on Shiloh Road and drive for two miles when it becomes Xavier Ave. The cemetery will be up the hill on the right.

Ghost Lore

Thanks to the movies, most people believe that every haunted place is located on a Native American burial ground. This is especially true when it deals directly with graveyards being placed over the top of older graveyards. For the most part, this belief is not valid, unless the place happens to be Vegors Cemetery. This historic hilltop cemetery overlooking the Boone and Des Moines rivers not only proves a challenge to find, it is also loaded with transplanted Native American graves.

- The ghosts of children will make themselves known by laughing at night.

- A portal to heaven will open for those who perform the correct ritual.

History

1849 – The cemetery was established by members of the area.

1861 – The one-year-old child of the Vegors family was buried in the cemetery.

1891 – C.H. Vegors died at the age of 44 years.

1894 – Emma Vegors died.

1911 – The memorial to Mrs. Henry Lott was constructed.

1960 – Remains of several people were reburied in the cemetery.

Investigation

The tall white statue in the cemetery is a memorial to Mrs. Henry Lott. The memorial was erected in 1911 by the Old Settlers Picnic Association of Bell's Mill. On the memorial to Mrs. Lott is an inscription that states that Lott died from exposure following an Indian raid. Lott was the first female white settler in Webster County.

According to the *History of Palo Alto County*, Henry Lott was an unsavory character who had a reputation for stealing horses and committing crimes and murders against many early settlers and Indians. Lott's history finally caught up with him when Chief Sidominadotah (a.k.a. Sintomniduta) was able to track several stolen horses back to the Lott residence. The Chief gave him an

opportunity to leave the county and never return. Unwisely, Lott did not take the opportunity to start afresh and refused to leave. Chief Sidominadotah made good on his threat and some tribe members came back and killed Lott's livestock, burned his cabin, and scared off his family.

Not being a stand-up type of guy, Lott took off and left his family. With no home, cattle, or food, along with being roughed up by the tribe, the Lott family had a difficult time with the elements. Lott's wife and children died a few days later due to exposure to the extreme cold. Upon hearing of this tragedy, Lott swore revenge upon the Sioux.

A few years later Lott returned to the area with his stepson and found Chief Sidominadotah and his tribe camping on a hunting expedition a short distance from where Lott was staying. Seeking his revenge, Lott managed to lure Sidominadotah away from the tribe and kill him. Later that evening Lott and his stepson dressed as Indians and came back and killed nearly all members of the tribe. Lott took what he could from the camp and burned the rest. The bodies were left where they were slaughtered.

Inside the cemetery is another historic monument that reads:

> In 1960, the bones of several pre-historic people of the region who were originally buried as a "bundle" on a hilltop southeast of the mouth of the Boone River were reburied in this cemetery.

Five separate Native American mounds are located in the cemetery. The cemetery contains a marker for the most northerly of the mounds.

Psychics who visit the cemetery report being overwhelmed with the feeling of Native American spirits still in the area.

Many visitors are surprised and startled to hear the sound of children laughing even though no children have been found in the cemetery.

The Dare. If you roll down the hill surrounding the cemetery three times, a portal to heaven will open up for you to go in.

Tara Bridge

Location: Tara, Webster County, Iowa
Former town of Tara (Now just outside of Fort Dodge)

Directions: From Fort Dodge take Hwy 169 north. Turn left on Hwy 7 west. Turn left on Johnson Ave. Turn right on 200th Street. Turn right on 210th Street. Turn left on Hayes Ave. Turn left on 220th Street and the bridge will be straight ahead.

Ghost Lore

Sometimes haunted places are so hard to find they really test an adventurer's patience and general navigation skills. Because the Tara Bridge is both secluded and partly in a town that no longer exists there, this place takes the cake. If you are able find this place you really deserve to see a ghost. Actually, you deserve a job with Rand McNally.

- An old bridge is haunted by the ghost of young children who were murdered by their mother.

- A bizarre, large, unknown creature inhabits the area of what was formerly the town of Tara.

- Vehicles traveling over the bridge will shut off until they safely reach the other side.

- If you travel to the bridge late at night you will hear the chilling eternal screams of the children who are forever roaming their death site.

History

1882 – Plans to form the town of Tara were initiated.

1882 – Two railroads came to the area.

1883 – The town of Tara was platted.

1893 – The Tara Junction and Tara Station were constructed.

1970s – Many of the buildings were still standing.

Currently – An ethanol plant purchased many of Tara's buildings, tore them down, and constructed a plant on the land. The plant is still operating there.

Investigation

The area was known by several names including Hinton Hollow and Dead Man's Hollow. The bridge is often called "Terror Bridge."

According to the *Douglas Township Historical Story* edited by Bernice Hicks and Ruby Woodbury, the story of the bridge being haunted goes way back to the late 1800s. The story goes that several farmers were in the fields haying when a fierce wind picked up, making it extremely difficult to work. One man flippantly cursed the wind in hopes that it would settle down and the men could then go back to work. However, he was not so lucky . . . as no sooner than the words left his mouth he fell to the ground dead.

Since the 1800s, residents have reported being chased through the area by a mysterious, howling ghost rider.

In an 1893 edition of the *Messenger* an article reports of the local curse. The story stated, "A party of ghost hunters from Ft. Dodge drove out to Tara last evening, spending time on the haunted bridge—they were told by the locals that the ghost was 'at home' from the 17th to the 25th."

An article by Deann Haden Luke republished an excerpt from Ray Flaherty's book *Our Lizard Creek Farm.* The excerpt reads, "One summer the rumor got around that there was a wild man living in our woods, seeking shelter from the rains either underneath the trees or under the railroad bridge."

Luke also reports of a woman, her son, and a friend who were traveling near Tara when they encountered an extremely large wild animal that ran past them at a high rate of speed. They were able to get a good look at the creature when it ran directly in front of them. What baffled the witnesses was that the creature was running on its hind legs.

Legend tells of a local Tara woman who went berserk and drove her children to the old railroad bridge. She calmly waited for an oncoming train to come by. Once the train was in sight she threw her children over the bridge down to the tracks. When the children were taken care of, she herself jumped onto the tracks. We were unable to find any information proving or disproving this event.

Visitors to the bridge report seeing the ghost of the woman still roaming the area where she met her death.

The Dare. If you venture out to the bridge at night and do not lock your windows and doors, the ghost of the woman will throw you off the bridge.

SOUTHEAST IOWA

Highway 34

Location: Burlington, Des Moines County, Iowa

Directions: Hwy 34 runs through Burlington.

Ghost Lore

We often take the U.S. highway system for granted. In years past highways provided the only means of traveling across the country. The advent of the interstate system made it possible to travel much easier from place to place. In fact, interstates have turned many local highways into ghost roads. However, the people of Burlington believe they actually have a ghost on their highway.

- An unearthly former slave forever roams the old Underground Railroad.

- A vanishing hitchhiker has been picked up along Highway 34.

History

1843 – Construction of the First Congregational Church began.

1843 – An Underground Railroad tunnel was constructed in the basement of the First Congregational Church.

1854 – The CB&Q came to Galesburg.

1855 – The CB&Q extended their railway into Burlington.

1867 – A bigger section of the church was constructed from an early English design incorporating a rust-colored limestone façade and exposed-stone buttresses along each side.

Investigation

The Underground Railroad was a system of secret underground tunnels in 14 northern states that provided escaped slaves a transportation route from the south to their freedom in the north.

Burlington was a hotbed for the railroad. According to an article by Jay Black, there is a narrow limestone tunnel running under the streets and sidewalks of Burlington. The tunnel was dug when Burlington served as a port city. The tunnel runs from Hawkeye Creek to a basement room at First Congregational Church. The slaves would hide out in town until they could head north to continue their quest for freedom under the cover of darkness.

One resident of Burlington played a big part in the Underground Railroad. Rev. William Salter served as the pastor of the First Congregational Church from 1846 to 1910. History shows that he was well-known for hiding slaves on his property and in his home.

Jay Black also dug up an interesting diary entry dating back to 1840 from the pastor of the First Congregational Church. It states: "Took up a collection (today) for the Amistad captives."

In addition to using the Underground Railroad, slaves also traveled on railroad cars that ran from Burlington up to Illinois on their way to Chicago.

Bruce Carlson wrote in his book *Ghosts of Des Moines County* that a courageous slave escaped from a plantation somewhere down south. The man is said to have traveled up north on the Underground Railroad eventually ending up in Burlington. While in Burlington the man had plans of starting his new life when he contracted diphtheria and died shortly after. It is suggested that the man was actually buried in the basement of an Underground Railroad safe house. This is not the end of his story, because even 140 years after his death the man is eternally seeking his freedom.

Carlson documents several sightings of a ghostly man carrying a leather bag walking along the road. One report is of a driver stopping to pick up a hitchhiker along the road. The driver asked the weary traveler where he was headed. The passenger stated that he was on his way to a 40-acre farm that he was never able to claim. The man looked away for a moment and when he looked back over, the seat was empty and the man was simply gone. The driver was completely baffled when he was unable to locate the man or his leather bag.

Sightings of the man usually occur between 1:00 a.m. and 2:00 a.m.

Many residents of Burlington are familiar with the story of the hitchhiker, yet few have had the opportunity for a personal viewing.

Stony Hollow Road

Location: Burlington, Des Moines County, Iowa

Directions: Take Hwy 99 from Burlington for approximately eight miles. Turn left on Stony Hollow Road. The bluffs will be a few hundred yards down the road.

Ghost Lore

Every town seems to have at least one road surrounded in legend and lore. Oftentimes these roads are situated somewhere out in the country, surrounded only by woods and mystery. Many of us pass over these old roads never knowing the unique history of the area they span. Even though most of these stories end up as nothing more than urban legends, those visiting Stony Hollow Road believe the history is responsible for its haunting.

During the late 1800s, a young maiden named Lucinda was secretly engaged to a young man from the area. They had made plans to meet one evening on the cliffs and run away to start their life together. Unfortunately, the young man never showed. Overcome and distraught, Lucinda could not fathom the thought of losing her love and she threw herself from cliffs to her death on the road below.

- Every year on the anniversary of her death the woman relives her tragic suicide.

- Saying the name of deceased woman (Lucinda) will invoke her spirit and bring about your own death.

History

During the 1800s the Stony Hollow area was known as Sherfey's Glen.

The Stony Hollow area was around in the 1900s.

A plat book shows several families owning land in the area, including Sherfey, Rand, Ohrt, Warth, and Eversmann.

Investigation

There are several different stories about Lucinda and her death. One version states that she was in love with a black man and her father had forbidden it. Realizing that the couple could never be together Lucinda took her life by jumping off of the cliffs.

Why did the young man not show up? One version states that he got his buggy wheel stuck in the mud and was unable to make the rendezvous. Bruce Carlson writes in *Ghosts of Des Moines County* that the young man never showed up and Lucinda went home only to awake the next day to hot gossip in the area that the young man had run away with a young woman from the nearby town. After hearing the devastating news Lucinda hurried off to their secret meeting space on the cliffs. Thinking that life was not worth living without her true love she jumped to her death.

Years ago residents reported seeing the ghost of a young woman running along the bluffs along Sherfey's Glen. It is believed that the ghost was that of Lucinda running the bluffs of the young couple's secret meeting area. The local legend states that Lucinda's ghost decided to spend eternity in the home of the love who abandoned her.

We searched the death records of Des Moines County from 1880-1890 and found no death record of any Lucinda. We were unable to find a death record of any young girl committing suicide during that time period. We also sought out children's names of those families who owned land near Sherfey's Glen. We found no names that matched or were similar to Lucinda.

Many of the residents of Burlington were familiar with the story of the ghost. One woman who grew up in the area told us that she had heard that if you drive out the area you will hear the sounds of a woman sobbing uncontrollably.

We spoke with several witnesses who reported seeing the ghost of a young woman out on Stony Hollow Road. The ghost often disappears when people approach.

The Dare. There are two dares at Stony Hollow Road.

The first is that if you speak Lucinda's name three times in a row, you will be cursed and die the next day.

The other dare is that if you try to climb the cliffs where Lucinda is said to have died, someone or something will not allow you to reach the top.

The Banshee of Brady Street

Location: Davenport, Scott County, Iowa

Directions: Brady Street runs through downtown Davenport.

Ghost Lore

You may think that the only way in which you can hear the wailing sounds of a Banshee is to visit Ireland. But don't purchase your ticket to the Emerald Isle just yet. It is much easier to visit the city of Davenport, because just like Ireland, many residents reported hearing the sounds of a Banshee wailing throughout the night.

A cursed house once stood along Brady Street bringing bad luck to all those who lived in it.

History

1918 – The Schachts purchased a large Victorian home on Brady Street.

1920s – Davenport was a heavily residential area.

Investigation

Jerome Pohlen, in his book *Oddball Iowa,* reports that soon after moving to Brady Street the Schachts family starting having extremely bad luck. While upstairs in the attic the seven-year-old boy "fell" out of the window and was impaled on a fence post. The daughter was unable to escape the family misfortune when she drowned in the bathtub. The family trouble didn't stop there. After losing her children, Mrs. Schachts decided to take her own life at the end of a rope in the basement. Maybe having the feeling that he lost everything, Alfred Schachts went into the kitchen and just as his wife did, ended up at the end of a rope. It should be noted that all of these deaths took place within one year.

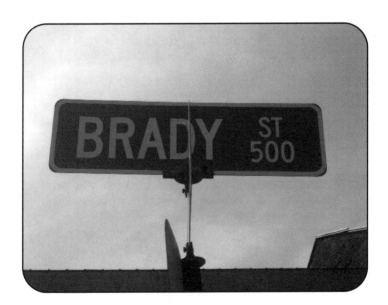

Pohlen also found that after all the mishaps, local realtors had a difficult time getting rid of the house. Finally a gangster took up the offer and brought up some of their molls from Chicago to run a bordello. The business did not last long as more and more customers stopped visiting the house.

Years later the house was used as boarding house for local college students. However, the house didn't remain quiet for long, and soon the students reported hearing strange noises and moans coming from the house. They also felt unexplained cold drafts in certain areas, covers were ripped from their beds, and mysterious figures appeared in the home. All the strange events were too much and students eventually moved out and the home started to deteriorate. Eventually the house was torn down and turned into a parking lot.

Ever since the house was torn down, the haunting activity seems to have moved to the streets and homes along Brady Street. It is along this street that residents report hearing the strange sounds of a Banshee. Loud screams and strange whistling are often reported.

There is a lot of speculation that the haunting activity is now focused on a single home on Brady Street, yet no one seems to know which exact house became cursed.

Old Police Station

Location: Davenport, Scott County, Iowa
Address: 226 West Fourth Street, Davenport, IA 52801-1308

Directions: From N. Harrison turn left on 3rd St. Then turn left on N. Main St. Turn left again on W. 4th St. and arrive at the City Hall.

Ghost Lore

A lot of times we visit a building without knowing its history. We may be able to name the previous business that called the building home, but our memory usually does not go too far back in time. Yet the people of Davenport remember when their City Hall building was their police station. Although the police station has long been moved to another building the spirits have not.

Ghosts of old prisoners, hanged on the site, continue to wait for their parole.

History

1894 to95 – The city hall building was constructed by J.W. Ross. The building cost $79,997.50 and was designed in the Richardsonian Romanesque style.

1874 – The town hall bell was built in Cincinnati to be used at an old fire station.

1896 – The town gathered for the dedication of the building.

1896 – The clock bell was moved from Cincinnati to the city hall building.

1980 – A $2.5 million renovation was undertaken.

1980 – The police station moved to another building across the street.

1986 – Don Neal who worked for the city fixed the city bell.

Investigation

The police station was originally in the city hall building. It has since been moved to another building across the street to Harrison Street.

Throughout the years, the 22 stained glass windows that were once the centerpiece of the building were removed and somehow lost.

Local lore tells that at one time the police station was located in the city hall building. Prisoners were housed in the station and when it came time for their punishment they did not have to travel far, as they were hanged up in the bell tower. We were unable to find any reports of hangings that took place in the building although we are still searching for more evidence.

Residents of the town often will walk by the building and look up into the old bell tower and are surprised to see the figure of a man hanging from a rope. When they look again the ghost is no longer there.

Another ghost in the building is said to be that of a heavyset man who was a regular visitor to the city council meetings. He has been seen walking around the building and often times witnesses report he is smoking a cigar.

We spoke with an employee who had heard of the building's haunted reputation yet had not had a paranormal experience.

The Black Angel of Oakland Cemetery

Location: Iowa City, Johnson County, Iowa
Address: Oakland Cemetery, 100 Brown Street, Iowa City, IA
Phone: (319) 356-5105

Directions: From Iowa Ave. turn left on N. Gilbert Street. Then turn right on E. Brown Street and you come to the cemetery.

Ghost Lore

When most people are asked to imagine a haunted place, they usually think of a cemetery. Haunted cemeteries are plastered all over movies, TV programs, and the Internet, so it comes as no surprise that most of us are not shocked to hear of a haunted cemetery. Yet how many of these haunted cemeteries can claim to house a black angel? Well, Oakland Cemetery can, and their Black Angel is surrounded by so much mystery and intrigue it should be on TV.

- Any woman who is kissed in front of the Black Angel will die within six months unless she is a virgin.

- Every Halloween the statue is said to turn a shade darker because of the souls it has taken throughout the year.

- If you touch the angel at exactly midnight you will die within seven years.

- If you stare directly into the statue at midnight you will suffer a fatal curse.

- The angel turned black because Teresa was a mean spirited person.

History

1836 – Teresa Feldevert was born in Bohemia.

Teresa and her son Eddie Dolezal moved to Iowa.

1843 – The Iowa Territorial Legislature deeded Oakland Cemetery to the people of Iowa City.

1891 – Eddie died of meningitis at the age of 18.

Teresa moved to Oregon and married Nicholas Feldevert.

1911 – Nicholas died and Teresa moved back to Iowa.

1911 – Teresa hired Bohemian artist Mario Korbel to design a monument for her son and husband.

1912 – The angel arrived at the cemetery. Eddie's gravestone was moved from its original spot to a spot next to the angel.

1917 – Iowa City purchased a block of land in the Woods Subdivision.

1919 – Christian Gaulocher donated 48 acres that included the Hickory Hill area.

1924 – Teresa died of cancer. Her ashes were buried under the angel.

1930 – The entry gates on Brown Street were added to the cemetery.

1934 – The concrete street system was installed.

1951 – Claude and Mabel Conklin Wood donated 40 acres.

1954 – The cemetery acquired its first backhoe which put an end to hand digging graves.

Investigation

The statue was constructed at a cost of over $5,000. According to some, there was a six-year disagreement over the statue that postponed its placement in the cemetery. The lawsuit was filed because Teresa believed the statue was missing a replica of her son's tree monument. A court case was said to have taken place with Teresa coming out of the losing end.

Why did the angel turn from bronze to black? There are many believed causes of the change in color from murder to storms. The main story circulating is that Teresa was a very mysterious woman who was interested in spells, magic and the like. Her evilness is said to have caused the statue to turn black.

Another version of the story states that a man constructed the statue over his wife's grave. However, due to her infidelity during their marriage the angel turned black as an eternal reminder of her sin. A small twist to the previous story involves a woman who had the angel erected for her deceased husband. The woman claimed that if she were ever unfaithful to her husband, the statue would turn black.

A popular story of the curse of the statue surrounds four young men who went into the cemetery and decided to urinate on the statue only to die in a car crash that evening.

Another story tells of a courageous young man who took a hacksaw to one of the statue's hands. Days later the man went insane and the authorities ended up finding his body in the Chicago River. The cause of death was strangulation and evidence left behind was a single thumbprint on his neck. It was said that a few days later a cemetery worker discovered a blackened piece of bronze that resembled the missing thumb of the statue. The statue is missing several fingers and a thumb.

Among the urban legends explaining the statue's color sits the scientific explanation that states the blackness is caused by the oxidation of the bronze due to the elements.

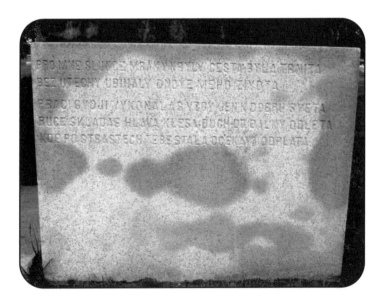

Teresa worked as a midwife. We found that Teresa was considered to be an odd woman by her neighbors, however we found no evidence that Teresa was an evil woman.

We spoke with the cemetery staff who informed us that hundreds of people trek to the cemetery each year to see the Black Angel. The statue has such lore that several weddings have even taken place at its base.

Although the statue has more than enough mystery surrounding it, there is one other part that continues to stir debate. Under the Black Angel is this inscription in an old Bohemian dialect that adds to the mystery of the statue. The inscription is this:

> PRO MNE SLUNCE MRAKY KRYLY GEST
> BYLA TRINTA NEZ UTEGHY UBIHALY
> DNOYE MEHO ZIYOTA PRAGI SYOJI
> VYKONALS UDZY JEN K DOBRU SUET
> RUCE SKLADAS HLAVA KLEASA DUGH M
> DALKY OKLETA KDE POSTRASTEGH
> TEBESTALA OCEKAYN ODPLATA

The most recent translation by university students and neighbors is this:

> The sun and clouds stood above my journey
> There were tough and joyful days in my life.
> You did my work just to make the world better.
> You fold your hands and your head goes down.
> Your spirit flies away where everlasting reward
> Is waiting for you after hardship

The Dare. If you have the courage to kiss the angel, you will die instantly.

The Blue Angel of Greenwood Cemetery

Location: Muscatine, Muscatine County, Iowa
Address: Greenwood Cemetery, 1814 Lucus Street,
Muscatine, IA
Phone: (563) 263-7051

Directions: Take 8th Street to Lucus Street which leads to the
cemetery. The Blue Angel is located in the back corner of the
graveyard.

Ghost Lore

Most of us believe that getting a rose is a good thing. Roses are
normally given to people as a gesture of appreciation, friendship,
empathy, infatuation, or love. So it comes as a big surprise that no
one would want to receive a rose from the Blue Angel. Well maybe
it is because if this angel gives you a rose it means that you will
soon meet the Grim Reaper.

- If the Blue Angel drops a rose in front of you, it means that you are cursed and are doomed to death.

- The statue will come alive in order to chase away vandals in the cemetery.

- Unknown footsteps will follow you through the cemetery.

History

1868 – Harry Huttig was born.

1868 – Kathryn Musser was born.

1935 – Harry Huttig passed away.

1948 – Kathryn Musser passed away.

1966 – The Chapel was placed on the National Register of Historic Places.

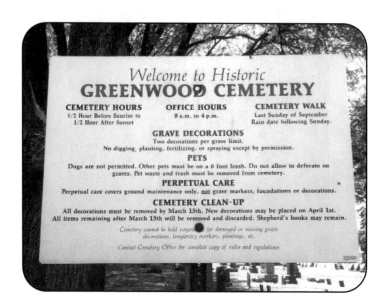

Investigation

The Blue Angel sits inside the mausoleum of Harry Huttig and Kathryn Musser. Originally the angel was constructed out of plaster and depicted an angel kneeling on the ground while holding a rose in her right hand.

The legend of the Blue Angel being haunted has been around for many years. Residents remember hearing it as far back as the 1940s.

The angel no longer holds a rose in her hand. Several years ago the statue was vandalized when someone cut off her hand. One popular legend explaining the vandalism is that a terrified resident thought that the only way to save others from suffering the curse of

the angel was to cut off her hand so she could not drop any more roses.

One man who lives near the cemetery wrote that the hand of the statue was not broken off in order to protect future visitors to the cemetery. He believes that a cemetery worker was doing routine maintenance on the mausoleum when the hand was accidentally broken off.

An article by John McCooley reported the account of a middle school student who believed that "On Halloween, at midnight, if she drops the rose, someone in your family will die."

Those who travel out to the cemetery at night to visit the statue are often amazed when they see a glowing rose being held in the angel's right hand even though it was cut off years ago.

We spoke with a lifelong resident who recalled hearing as a child that if you peek into the window and see a tear on this angel you will meet death.

There are numerous competing legends that surround the angel. The first theory states that if the angel turns blue while you are there, then you will be blessed with good luck. However, if the statue comes alive during your visit, you will die.

The statue is positioned in front of a blue cobalt glass window causing the statue to take on a blue hue when the sun shines in.

The statue may not be the only thing haunting the cemetery, as many visitors report the overwhelming feeling of being watched by something unseen.

Those who enter the graveyard will hear the sounds of footsteps following them. Startled, the visitors spin around to find that no one is following them.

New Virginia Cemetery

Location: New Virginia, Warren County, Iowa

Directions: From New Virginia travel toward Hwy. 35. The cemetery will be on the right.

Ghost Lore

This old cemetery houses some of New Virginia's first settlers, yet unlike many pioneer cemeteries, the New Virginia Cemetery is not located in a secluded woods out in the middle of nowhere. This cemetery is located right off the main road. Yet one man buried in the cemetery is still not happy with his grave's location and is set on making his anger known to all those who visit there.

- Mysterious lights have been seen roving through the grave-yard.

- The cemetery is haunted by the town's first resident.

History

1804 – John Felton was born.

1825 – John Felton married Miss Margaret Wootring.

1854 – Felton moved to the area that would become New Virginia.

1854 – Eliza Jane Stickel was the first person known to be buried in the New Virginia Cemetery.

1855 – The Methodist church of New Virginia was organized before the town was even established. The founding members included John Felton and his wife, Julia Knotts, Matilde Strock, William Reed and his wife, Nancy Felton, and Absalom Sayers.

1855 – John Felton built the first house in New Virginia.

1856 – The town of New Virginia was laid out.

1858 – The Post Office of New Virginia opened.

1859 – The town plot was recorded. It was owned by John Felton, Francis Reed, Absalom Knotts, and Joseph Knotts.

1863 – The church was built at a cost of $2,500. The church was also dedicated by Rev. E.M.H. Fleming.

1881 – A small railroad was in New Virginia.

1882 – Many residents of New Virginia made their living raising horses.

1882 – John Felton passed away.

1887 – The first issue of the *New Virginian* came out.

1901 – The City of New Virginia was formally incorporated.

1938 – The death of a traveler is said to have been recorded.

1953 – A gravestone for the unknown pioneer was constructed.

Investigation

Many of the first settlers of the area were from the state of Virginia, hence the name New Virginia.

Because he was one of the first settlers of the area, many people wrongly think it is the ghost of John Felton that is haunting the cemetery. When Felton was alive he owned 106 acres and served as assessor, town trustee, and justice of the peace. Needless to say Felton was well respected in the community.

Yet the real haunting belongs to someone no one knows. According to the *Cemetery and Death Records of Warren County, Iowa,* the first death in New Virginia was an unknown man. Records state that the stranger was passing through the area when he fell ill and passed away.

Another version of the story is that the man was part of a group traveling through the area in a covered wagon. When he fell ill his fellow travelers had no choice but to leave him in the hands of the local hotel where he died.

Yet another version of the story circulates telling of Alonzo Sayre, who is believed to be the pioneer man who died at the residence of William Reed in 1838. The man was then brought to the top of a hill and buried in the area that would become the New Virginia Cemetery.

Regardless of what version of the story is correct, the townspeople felt he needed a proper burial. In 1953, the town gathered a collection to purchase a gravestone for the unknown man. The inscription on the stone reads:

> An unknown Pioneer Man
> First burial in this
> Cemetery, 1854
> Erected, 1953
> By Kind Hearted People

The good residents of New Virginia also constructed another monument in the cemetery. A soldier's monument sits on the west side of the cemetery drive. The inscription on the stone reads:

> In memory of the Soldiers Who Gave Their All
> for Home, Fireside and Liberty. Erected by the
> citizens of New Virginia and Community.

Local stories tell that if you visit the cemetery at midnight you will see a glowing light hovering over the gravestone of the unknown pioneer. It is said that the man is upset with the community for changing his original grave and giving him the new marker in 1953.

River Road Park

Location: Wapello, Louisa County, Iowa

Directions: Take Main Street to the south, turn right on Fred Brown Street and you will arrive at the park.

Ghost Lore

Parks represent a chance for people to escape the concrete jail. People visit the park to enjoy green grass, open fields, or a heavily forested area. A lot of people just like to reconnect with the natural world, yet those who visit South End Park believe they are experiencing more supernatural than natural.

History

1990 – The City of Wapello purchased 80 acres of land for the cost of $62,100.

1991 – The city was given a Reap grant that helped fund the park.

Investigation

The park is also referred to as the South End Park.

The city had to remove the soccer fields because of a clause against organized sports in the conditions of the Reap grant.

The park also houses the city's sewage lagoons. It is claimed that this is the only park with the waste facilities in the state of Iowa.

At night those who enter the park will hear unknown sounds of chanting even though no source can be found.

We spoke with several residents who had heard of the haunting but did not have a personal experience.

This case is still under investigation.

Stoneking Cemetery

Location: Williamson, Lucas County, Iowa

Directions: Follow W South Ave. Take your first left on 280th Ave. which becomes 545. Turn right on 547th St. Turn right at 330th (there will be a small bridge to your right). Follow 330th to the cemetery.

Ghost Lore

Haunted cemeteries in the movies and on TV are almost always located in a secluded area far out in the woods away from any city. Many of the gravestones in these cemeteries are unmarked, overrun by weeds, and date back to the 1800s. Local residents are all famil-iar with the stories of the haunted cemetery. Well, these types of cemeteries only exist in the movies right? Wrong. The above description provides an accurate description of the Stoneking Cemetery. Just make sure you do not take up Joseph's invitation to join him in death.

- The cemetery is so eerie it was featured in the original *Children of the Corn* movie.

- A cryptic message on a gravestone beckons visitors to join the occupant.

- If visitors spot a specific ghost in the cemetery, they will die.

History

1849 – Joseph Stoneking was born.

1916 – Mr. Stoneking passed away.

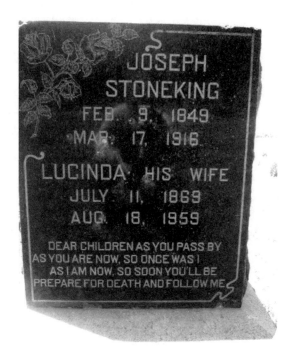

Little is known about the cemetery. What is known is that several Stonekings are buried in the cemetery. The Stoneking family was among the first settlers in the area.

The area was once known as Stoneking.

Investigation

The Cemetery is also known as the Oak Hill Cemetery.

Although the first *Children of the Corn* movie was filmed in Hornick, Salix, Sioux City, and Whiting, Iowa, the Stoneking Cemetery was not featured in the movie. Actually no cemeteries appear in the movie. We will leave it up to you to sit through the six mediocre *Children of the Corn* sequels to see if the cemetery makes an appearance.

The oldest gravestone in the cemetery dates back to 1865. We found several other gravestones dating back to the 1800s.

The gravestone with the mysterious inscription is that of Joseph Stoneking. There are several circulating versions as to what the inscription actually says. The inscription reads:

> DEAR CHILDREN AS YOU PASS BY
> AS YOU ARE NOW, SO ONCE WAS I
> AS I AM NOW, SO SOON YOU'LL BE
> PREPARE FOR DEATH AND FOLLOW ME

Many people have spotted the ghost of Joseph Stoneking throughout the cemetery. However, you may want to skip your sighting of Joseph as local lore tells that if you see the ghost of Joseph while you are in the cemetery, you will die shortly after.

Several residents told the story of a young man who visited the cemetery and was startled to see a male ghost near the Stoneking grave. The man is said to have been killed in a motorcycle accident one week later.

Unexplained lights have also been reported moving through the cemetery at night.

SOUTHWEST IOWA

The Black Angel of Fairview Cemetery

Location: Council Bluffs, Pottawattamie County, Iowa
Address: Fairview Cemetery, 209 Pearl Street, Council Bluffs, IA 51503-0826
Phone: (712) 328-4651

Directions: From West Broadway head toward 8th St. Turn Right onto Pearl St.

The angel is located in Section H of the cemetery.

Ghost Lore

The average person spends one-third of their life sleeping. During sleep most of us dream; it is a normal part of sleeping. For years, psychologists have debated the purpose and meaning of dreams, without clear-cut answers. Unfortunately, we often have very little control over the type of dreams that we have. Many of us also have reoccurring dreams, but how many of us have dreams that end up killing us?

- Water flowing from the fountain will cause immediate death.

- The mesmerizing eyes of the statues will follow you as you walk by.

- Those brave enough to stare into her eyes will fall dead within 24 hours.

- The statue refuses to keep its bronze coloring regardless of how many times it is polished.

History

1833 – Ruth Anne Brown was born.

Mormons first used the high ridge of Fairview as a cemetery.

1846 – The Fairview Cemetery was officially opened.

1854 – Ruth Anne married Grenville M. Dodge in Salem, Massachusetts.

1880 – Iowa law required the recording of deaths.

1916 – Ruth Anne Dodge died in her home in New York City. Her body was brought to Council Bluffs where she was buried in Fairview Cemetery.

Ruth's two daughters, Miss Anne Dodge and Mrs. Frank Pusey commissioned Daniel Chester French to create a statue of the angel that appeared to Ruth in a vision. The statue took more than two years to complete at a cost exceeding $40,000.

1919 – Water was turned on in the fountain.

1920 – A private ceremony was held to dedicate the statue.

1958 – A group of Girl Scouts proposed painting the statue black. Fortunately it did not pass.

1960 – The water to the fountain was shut off.

1964 – The care of the statue was transferred to the City Park Board.

1965 – The Park Board looked into moving the statue to the Dodge House in town. No action was taken.

1978 – The Park Board once again considered moving the statue and once again no action was taken.

1980 – For the final time the Board tried and failed to move the statue.

1980 – The Angel was listed as a historic site on the National Register of Historic Places.

1985 – The statue received a major restoration costing $5,000.

1987 – A big celebration was held for the newly restored statue.

Investigation

Ruth Dodge began having an odd dream. In her dream she encountered a beautiful winged woman whom she took to be an angel. The woman approached her through a foggy mist on a boat carrying a small bowl under one arm. The woman offered Ruth something to drink. The strange angel spoke to her saying, "I bring you both a promise and a blessing." The bizarre dream came to her three straight nights. On the third night Ruth accepted the angel's cryptic offer for a drink. When she awoke in the morning her daughters noticed that she seemed much calmer than normal. She stated that she felt transformed into a new and glorious being. However, misfortune soon followed as by the end of the day, Ruth had passed away.

The man who constructed the angel, Daniel French, went on to sculpt the famous statue of the president in the Lincoln Memorial.

The monument bears this inscription:

> Blessed are the Pure in Heart, for they shall see God – Matt 5:8
>
> And he showed me a pure river of the water of life: clear and crystal, proceeding out of the throne of God and of the Lamb – Rev. 22:1
>
> Let him that is athirst come and whosoever will, let him take of the water of life freely – Rev. 22:17

Several witnesses claim to have seen the angel flying around the cemetery late at night.

Many people feel that if you pass by the angel, you will be forever cursed with ill health.

A group of paranormal investigators claimed that they were at the cemetery investigating the statue when they noticed the "tears" of the statue. The group believed the tears only to be moisture caused by precipitation or dew falling from the statue's face.

The Dare. If you grab the hand of the angel you will meet your fate, as she will lead you into death.

Historic General Dodge House

Location: Council Bluffs, Pottawattamie County, Iowa
Address: 605 South Third Street, Council Bluffs, IA 51503-6614
Phone: (712) 322-3504
Museum Hours: Tues. to Sat.: 10-5, Sun.: 1-5. Closed January
Admissions: Adults: $7, Seniors (62+): $5, Youth: $3, Children under 6: Free

Directions: Take Pearl St. which becomes S. Main St. Turn left on Story St. Then turn Right on S. 3rd St. and the home will appear ahead.

Ghost Lore

A home provides more than simple protection from the elements. Homes are an extension of ourselves and they often reflect the owners' interests and personalities. So it comes as no surprise that people become attached to them. But can a person become so attached to his home that he refuses to leave even after death? That is exactly what some visitors to General Dodge's Historic Home believe. Once you tour this magnificent Victorian home, you may also believe that no one would ever leave it.

- The ghost of General Dodge has not left the house he loved so much.

- Unexplained globes of light are spotted near the home.

- Strange noises have been reported in the front yard of the home.

History

1831 – Grenville Dodge was born in Massachusetts to Sylvanus and Julia Dodge.

1852 – Dodge graduated from Norwich University.

1852 – Dodge became surveyor for the Rock Island Railroad.

1854 – He married Ruth Anne Brown in Massachusetts.

1855 – Dodge moved to Council Bluffs.

1855 – The Dodge's first daughter, Lettie, was born.

1858 – A second daughter named Ella was born.

1861 to 1865 – Gen. Dodge fought in the Civil War. He enjoyed immediate success as a soldier and commander, establishing a spy network for Gen. Ulysses S. Grant.

1866 – A third child named Anna was born.

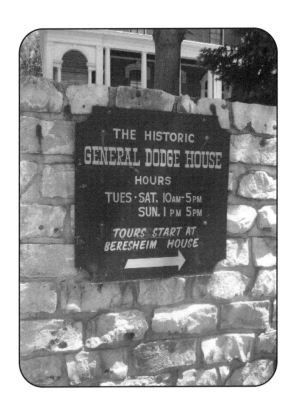

1869 – The Dodge house was completed.

1870 – Dodge and his family moved into the house on Third Street.

1870 to 1900 – Dodge worked as a railroad man for more than a dozen companies.

1916 – Dodge died in his home at Council Bluffs.

1961 – The Dodge house was designated a National Historic Landmark by the United States Department of the Interior.

1963 – The home was purchased by the Council Bluffs Park Board, the Historical Society of Pottawattamie County, and local residents and businesses.

1964 – The home's preservation was placed in the hands of a board of trustees.

Investigation

The elegant Victorian home cost over $35,000 to construct. The three-story, 14-room home overlooks the Missouri River.

The haunting activities are usually blamed on the ghost of General Dodge. Lore tells that Gen. Dodge refuses to leave his former house because he loved it so much.

Gen. Dodge is considered by many to be the greatest railroad builder of all time.

We spoke with the historic home's director who had been at the home for 10 years and had no personal experiences in the home.

Several employees were working in the home when they heard the sounds of pots and pans rattling in the kitchen. Realizing that no one was in the kitchen, the employees decided to investigate. However once they got to the room they could not find any cause for the noises.

The most-often-reported ghost is that of a woman seen roaming the home in a white nursing gown.

Several musicians who play at the home picked up the sense that the head servants' room is haunted.

Another employee was walking through the kitchen when the stovepipe suddenly fell off as though some unseen force had pushed it.

Visitors report hearing the sounds of two men arguing out in the middle of the street, yet when they go to the noise, no one is around.

Union Pacific Museum

Location: Council Bluffs, Pottawattamie County, Iowa
Address: 200 Pearl Street, Council Bluffs, IA 51503-0825

Directions: From West Broadway travel toward 8th St. Turn onto Pearl St.

Ghost Lore

If you miss the romance and adventure of the passenger train then the Union Pacific Museum is perfect for you. Filled with old train cars, historical information, and more train details that you could ever ask for, the museum will steam-power you back to a time when the train dominated the rails. Visitors can spend hours at the museum walking among the exhibits, getting the spirit of the railways. However, others are more interested in seeing the real spirits haunting the museum.

223

- When the building housed the public library, the basement was the place of many odd occurrences.

- A ghostly spirit has been sighted in the museum's stairwell.

History

1859 – President Lincoln visited the home of the Hon. W.H.M. Pusey. The home stood where the museum is now located.

1862 – President Lincoln signed the Pacific Railroad Act that created the Union Pacific Railroad.

1866 – The group known as the Young Men's Library Association sought to create a library.

1869 – Several residents including Professor Armstrong and Horace Everett created the High School Library Association.

1871 – The group named the Public School Library was incorporated.

1873 – The Public School Library merged with the YMCA. and located in the Woodbury building. W.T. Robinson was appointed as the first librarian.

1875 – The city tried to levy a tax for the support of the library. The levy attempt failed.

1878 – With many of the books being lost and worn, the Council Bluffs Library Association was formed to revamp the library.

1882 – The Free Public Library was opened to the public.

1889 – The library was moved to the Merriam Block.

1905 – A Chicago firm was granted a contract to build the new library with local residents J.C. and W. Woodward selected as architects. The design was for a three-story building at a cost of $88,160.55.

1905 – The new building was dedicated with a speech by General Dodge.

2003 – The Union Pacific Railroad Museum opened.

Currently – Over 25,000 visitors tour the museum each year.

Investigation

The building that now houses the museum was originally used for the public library. Many strange things took place in basement of the library including books that would fly off the shelves on their own and other objects that were said to mysteriously appear and disappear.

The cause of the haunting at the museum is believed to be a former woman of Council Bluffs. The most widely believed history of the woman is that she was a local pianist during the 1800s. For some unknown reason she was an outcast in the community and continues to walk the area where she once lived. The woman is said to be clothed in an elegant Victorian dress.

We spoke with the museum director who informed us that there have been numerous mysterious events that have transpired at the museum. Although he has never had a personal experience, he believes that the ghost of the museum is a friendly one.

One of the most haunted places of the museum is the stairwell. It is there that several staff members and visitors have seen the ghost of a woman walking down the stairs. The woman is described as being clothed in Victorian dress.

The northwest corner of the museum is also believed to be haunted. Museum staffers have passed by the surveyor's tent exhibit only to find the tent flapping from some mysterious unseen force.

Unexplainable noises have been reported throughout the museum. These noises are described as a strange humming or fluttering sound.

Senior volunteers at the museum remembered being afraid to go into the basement of the library when they were children.

Many of the museum's volunteers had heard the story of the place being haunted.

Saint Mary's Cemetery

Location: Hamburg, Fremont County, Iowa

Directions: From Argyle Street, turn onto Bluff Street. Turn right onto P Street and stay to the right on Mt. Lookout Road.

Ghost Lore

Many cemeteries have statues. From angels to saints they are a common sight throughout the country. While some of these statues have a meaning behind them, others are simply for show. But more and more of these statues are taking on the lore of being haunted. This is certainly the case in St. Mary's Cemetery.

- Unknown weeping has been heard coming from the memorial.

- A mysterious woman has been seen at the foot of the statues.

History

1850 – Father Christian Hoecken traveled to the French Village. (Just northeast of where Hamburg sits today.)

1850 – Clement Lamoureaux and Louis Trudeau, along with their families were the founding members of St. Mary's Parish.

1874 – The St. Mary's Parish constructed their church.

1880 – The parish acquired the land for a cemetery.

1885 – Father A. Cook blessed the new cemetery and gave it the name of St. Mary's.

1885 – The first official burial took place in the cemetery. Church records indicate it was a nine-year-old named Anna Gordon.

1886 – The cemetery acquired a new strip of land to be used for a road.

Investigation

The cemetery's proper name is St. Mary's Catholic Cemetery.

The cemetery was consecrated on All Soul's Day.

It is believed that two of the founding members of the church, John Lamoureaux and Joseph Valandre, are buried in the cemetery even though they passed away in 1870.

The three large stone figures that are reported to be haunted serve as a memorial to the Burkhiser children buried in the cemetery.

Many visitors stop by the memorial only to hear an eerie wailing that sounds like it is coming from the statue themselves.

A mysterious figure of a woman has been seen kneeling at the feet of the statues. When approached, the "woman" appears to simply vanish into thin air.

Tedrow Cemetery

Location: Mount Ayr, Ringgold County, Iowa

Directions: From Hwy 2 take County Hwy P64 south (right), take a right on 260th Street (dirt road). Follow road then take first right (unmarked dirt road).

Ghost Lore

Rural cemeteries pose a challenge. You first must get directions to the cemetery. Next, you have to hope your directions are accurate. After that you can venture to the site, check it out, and hopefully experience some paranormal activity. When you have had your fill you can leave the cemetery and return to the safety of your own home. Yet those visiting the Tedrow Cemetery believe that the cemetery will not let you leave.

- A strange glowing light is often spotted hovering through the cemetery.

- Regardless of the temperature in the surrounding area, the cemetery will always be cold.

- A tree with an evil face haunts the cemetery.

History

Not much is known about the history of this pioneer cemetery, which may add to its lore.

Betty Ruby and Ruth Haley of the Ringgold County Historical Society Diagonal produced a list of those buried in the cemetery.

1844 – Tedrow Cemetery land was deeded to T.V. Burtch. It had been used for burials since the early 1840s and was originally known as Spring Hill Cemetery.

1872 – It was acquired by the Dover Township trustee and renamed Tedrow Cemetery.

2000 – Rick Wiley updated the cemetery list.

2010 – In July, 38 of the 54 headstones were shattered by vandals.

Investigation

Many people refer to the cemetery as Ted's Row cemetery, while the official name is Tedrow Cemetery.

Tedrow Cemetery is considered a pioneer cemetery. Iowa law defines a "Pioneer Cemetery" as one in which there have been no more than six burials in the past 50 years.

Tales of the rural cemetery being haunted have been circulating for at least 25 years. We spoke with many residents that were all famil-iar with the haunting activity that takes places out at the cemetery. One witness told us that he was out at the cemetery at night when he noticed a dark figure near the tree staring at him. Unable to make out exactly what the figure was, the man quickly exited the cemetery.

According to local lore the cemetery is not the only haunted thing in the area; the trees surrounding the cemetery are also believed to be haunted. One tree in particular is said to have an evil face on it. Ghostly moans have also been heard drifting through the trees. Teenagers tell stories of mysterious cults performing strange cere-monies inside the cemetery.

The Dare. Drive into the cemetery and turn off your vehicle and lights. Soon you'll see a shadow run past you and your car will not start, trapping you in the cemetery.

The Axe Murder House

Location: Villisca, Montgomery County, Iowa
Address: 508 East Second Street, Vilisca, IA 50864-1111
Mailing Address: The Villisca Axe Murder House/Olson Linn Museum, 323 East Fourth Street, Villisca, IA 50864-1146
Phone: (712) 621-4291
Website: www.villiscaiowa.com
Email: dmlinn@mddc.com

Directions: Corner of Sixth Ave S and E Second Street.

Ghost Lore

Americans tend to have a macabre sense of curiosity when it comes to murder. Many serial killers become household names and border on being celebrities. From prison they receive marriage proposals, fan mail, and even offers to purchase their artwork. Yet the communities in which the crimes took place are more eager to forget than to embrace their past. If you are the type of traveler who likes to seek out the landmarks where such horrific crimes were committed, you may have a hard time because the communities are quick to erase any evidence of the crimes. Sometimes the place "accidentally" catches fire like Ed Gein's house or is torn down like Jeffrey Dahmer's apartment complex. Very few places actually preserve and promote their sinister history, yet the Axe Murder House is one of those few places.

- A family murdered in the house still remains there.

- Unknown figures have been spotted wandering the home.

- Those brave enough to spend the night in the home report seeing a door open and close on its own.

- A piece of a victim's head was stolen from the crime scene.

- Ghosts of the murdered children pinch, push, and shove, unsuspecting visitors.

History

1868 – The home was built by George Loomis.

1889 – Josiah Moore married Sarah Montgomery.

1903 – Josiah Moore purchased the home.

1908 – Josiah opened his own store with a John Deere franchise.

1912 – The Moore family and two overnight guests were killed in the family home.

1912 to 1915 – The home remained in the Moore family.

1915 – J.H. Geesman purchased the house.

1920 to 1940s – The home had several different owners.

1940s – The home was renovated with the addition of electricity and plumbing.

1960s – Villisca State Savings and Loan owned the home.

1971 – Darwin Kendrick was listed as the owner of the historic home.

1994 – The Murder House was sold to Rick and Vicki Sprague.

1994 – Darwin and Martha Linn purchased the home.

1994 – The Linns renovated the home to its original state with new paint, new wiring and plumbing.

1997 – The Moore home received Iowa's Preservation at its Best award.

1998 – The home was placed on the National Register of Historic Places.

Investigation

On June 10, 1912, the little sleepy town of Villisca got a horrific wakeup call. The town was abuzz with talk of the previous night's events. Residents could not believe that they had a murderer

among them. For Josiah Moore, his family, and Lena and Ina Stillinger the news came too late as their bodies were found at the Moore family home.

The Murders

During the fateful morning the house was full of people. In the house was Josiah, his wife Sarah, their children Herman, Katherine, Boyd, and Paul. Unfortunately, the Moore children had their two friends Lena and Ina Stillinger sleeping over that night. The killer (or killers) stealthy moved from room to room ending the life of each person with a bloody axe.

The bodies were found between 8:00 a.m. and 8:30 a.m. However only one deputy was watching the house and when word spread many curious townsfolk rushed through the three doors leading into the house, disrupting the evidence. The axe was found leaning against a basement wall.

Dr. J. Clark Cooper, the coroner who worked on the case, reported that the bodies of the children were all found facedown on the bed. Other reports state that all the bodies were also completely covered with bedclothes and clothing. Other odd things were noticed such

as the mirror being covered by a bedspread and all the curtains had been pulled shut.

It is believed that the adults represented the biggest threat and were therefore killed first. Evidence suggests that the rest of the victims were killed in their sleep.

A local pool hall owner by the name of Bert McCaull was said to have taken a piece of Moore's skull back to his business wrapped in yellow paper.

The Suspects

The murders have been documented in full detail in several books, a documentary video, and numerous websites. The only thing missing from all the research is the identity of the murderer. Even though no one was ever convicted there were plenty of suspects including:

Reverend George Kelly. Rev. Kelly was a traveling preacher who settled down in Iowa in 1912. In 1917, Rev. Kelly was arrested and charged with the murder at the Axe Murder House. Even with a confession that was later retracted, the trial ended in a hung

jury. Kelly was retried, and this time he was acquitted. Why was he charged? Well, Kelly traveled to Villisca for a children's day at the Presbyterian Church the night before the murders occurred and he left the next morning.

Frank Jones. Frank was Josiah Moore's boss for several years until Josiah left his job to start his own implement company. Josiah also took with him a very profitable John Deere franchise contract. Jones was said to be visibly upset about the betrayal. It didn't help that it was rumored that Moore was having an affair with Jones' daughter-in-law. Jones was accused of hiring a hit man to kill Moore, yet he was never arrested or charged and denied any involvement in the crime.

William Mansfield. William was the hit man who was said to be hired by Frank Jones. Obviously William's reputation as cocaine-addicted serial killer didn't help his cause. Add in the speculation

that William was responsible for the axe murder of his wife and family and you have the perfect suspect. Unlike other suspects, William was actually arrested and later released for lack of evidence. He was eventually awarded over $2,000 in a wrongful arrest lawsuit.

Miscellaneous. Residents of the town also put forth their own theories including a traveling serial killer, a hobo, and a crazed maniac. None of these theories ever panned out, and the case is still unsolved.

The Haunting

The home has been investigated by numerous paranormal research groups from around the United States. Many of these groups have claimed to have captured the voices (EVP) of the children, the killer, and Josiah and Sarah Moore.

A group from Missouri claimed to have captured a photograph of the killer while investigating the home.

Numerous other photographs are said to have captured unusual balls of light.

A visitor spent the night in the house and reported feeling a strong pressure on his chest.

Many visitors report getting unexplained cold chills while spending time in the home.

Visitors who spend time in the home have reported seeing the door to the children's room open and close on its own.

While giving tours, the owners have witnessed many paranormal events. The tour groups have experienced furniture moving on its own, unknown voices, lamps refusing to stay on, and unknown figures roaming through the house.

The owner told us of a young boy who was visiting the home with his father. The curious boy started to wander the home and eventually ended upstairs. When he came back downstairs he told his father that the man upstairs had touched him. Knowing that no one was upstairs the father asked the boy who had touched him. The boy looked up at as though he saw someone standing there, pointed to the staircase and said "he did." The confused father looked at the staircase but saw no one.

One of the more bizarre reports of activity in the house revolved around several visitors who had seen what appeared to be blood dripping from the walls. However, when the shocked witnesses tried to investigate the mysterious phenomenon, the blood was simply gone.

Several visitors touring the home reported that while they call out to the children they are often pushed, pinched, or shoved by some unseen force.

One visitor was upstairs and had sat down on the bed and started calling out for a response from one of the children when he felt a tug on his pant leg. He looked under the bed to find the source of the tug, but was shocked to find nothing under the bed.

The Dare. Spend the entire evening in the home and you will witness the murders being replayed as though they are happening that evening.

Roseman Bridge

Location: Winterset, Madison County, Iowa

Directions: Take John Wayne Drive to Summit. Turn onto Summit which becomes Hwy. 92. Follow 92 east and turn left on Roseman Bridge Road then follow the signs.

Ghost Lore

For some of you, the thought of reading through the sappy romance book—or sitting through the equally sappy movie—*The Bridges of Madison County* is terrifying. For others the terrifying part starts when they visit the haunted bridge in Madison County.

- A man hanged for theft still haunts the bridge.

- Strange, high-pitched noises seem to emanate from the bridge.

243

- A man being chased by a posse simply disappeared on the bridge.

History

1883 – The Roseman Bridge was constructed.

1892 – Local lore tells of a man hanged on the bridge for theft.

1954 – The Roseman Bridge was renovated.

1970s – The bridge was still open for vehicle traffic.

1992 – The bridge was renovated again at a cost of over $150,000.

1994 – A movie crew arrived in Winterset to film *The Bridges of Madison County.*

1994 – For the movie, the bridge was redesigned to look as it did in 1965.

Investigation

At one time Madison County had 19 covered bridges. When Robert James Waller's book *The Bridges of Madison County* came out only seven of the bridges were still in existence.

To make the Roseman Bridge seem more rural and rustic, lights were added during the filming of the movie. However, the lights were removed as soon as filming was complete. If seeing the haunted bridge is not enough for you, pieces of the bridge that were replaced during renovation are available at the gift shop next to the bridge.

The real history of the haunting of Roseman Bridge is still unknown. There are several versions of the original story.

One version tells of a young man who fell in love with a local girl. The girl's father did not approve of the relationship and framed the young man for theft as a way to split them up. The young man's fate was a public hanging down on Roseman Bridge.

The second version involves a local posse that was in hot pursuit of a fugitive. After some chasing the posse finally managed to surround the man at Roseman Bridge. The posse split up and slowly walked into the bridge from both sides. As the men approached, they suddenly heard an ear-splitting, high-pitched scream and noticed that the suspect had mysteriously vanished. When the shocked men came to the middle of the bridge, it was terrifyingly cold.

We are unsure what actually happened at the site during and prior to 1892. We do know that since that time people have reported the Roseman Bridge as being haunted.

We spoke with a lifelong resident who informed us that he has heard the stories of the man haunting the bridge since his childhood.

Many local residents still report hearing strange noises coming from the bridge even though it is under constant surveillance.

NUMBERS

A

B

Y

Chad Lewis is a paranormal investigator for Unexplained Research LLC, with a Master's Degree in Applied Psychology from the University of Wisconsin-Stout. Chad has spent years traveling the globe researching ghosts, strange creatures, crop formations, and UFOs. Chad is a former state director for the Mutual UFO Network and has worked with BLT Research on crop circle investigations. Chad is the organizer of the *Unexplained* Conferences and hosted *The Unexplained* paranormal radio talk show and television series.

Terry Fisk is also a paranormal investigator for Unexplained Research LLC and lecturer on death and the afterlife. He is a shamanic Buddhist practitioner and member of the Foundation for Shamanic Studies who studied Philosophy and Religion at the University of Wisconsin. Terry co-hosted *The Unexplained* paranormal radio talk show and directed *The Unexplained* television series. He has investigated hauntings with famed medium Allison DuBois and TV psychic Chip Coffey.

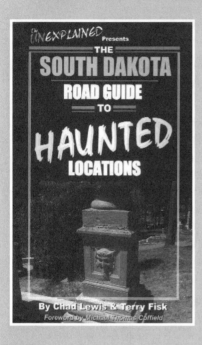

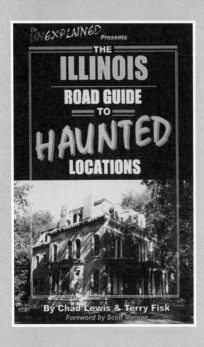

The UNEXPLAINED
Presents

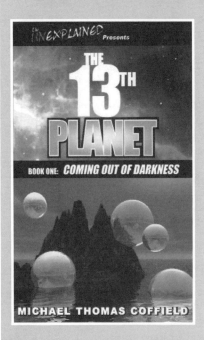

HIDDEN HEADLINES

Strange, Unusual, & Bizarre Newspaper Stories 1860- 1910

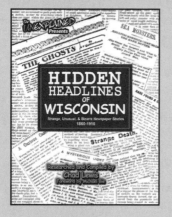

HIDDEN HEADLINES OF WISCONSIN
by Chad Lewis
Foreword by Michael Bie

- YAWNS HERSELF TO DEATH
- FARMER SHOT AN ALLIGATOR
- CHICKEN HAS HUMAN FACE
- TOADS TUMBLE FROM SKY

ISBN: 978-0-9762099-6-6

HIDDEN HEADLINES OF NEW YORK
by Chad Lewis

- ATE A QUART OF GRASSHOPPERS
- A PETRIFIED GIANT
- SEA SERPENT SPOTTED
- GREEN GOATS WITH RED LEGS
- HALF HUMAN-HALF MONKEY

ISBN: 978-0-9762099-9-7

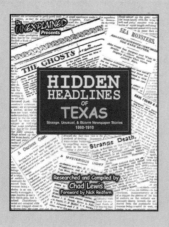

HIDDEN HEADLINES OF TEXAS
by Chad Lewis
Foreword by Nick Redfern

- GHOSTS IN THE ALAMO
- LEMONADE DEATH
- EIGHTEEN-HORN COW
- A MONSTER RATTLESNAKE

ISBN: 978-0-9762099-8-5

the UNEXPLAINED
Presents

"The Unexplained" Sweatshirt

COLOR: Black
SIZES: M, L, XL, 2XL

Hooded. 100% cotton. "The Unexplained with Chad Lewis and Terry Fisk" on front.

"The Unexplained" Tee shirt

COLOR: Black
SIZES: M, L, XL, 2XL

Short-sleeved. 100% cotton. "The Unexplained with Chad Lewis and Terry Fisk" on front.

www.unexplainedresearch.com

Unexplained Research LLC
P.O. Box 2173
Eau Claire, WI 54702-2173
www.unexplainedresearch.com
admin@unexplainedresearch.com